HEBREWS

A CALL TO COMMITMENT

HEBREWS

A CALL TO COMMITMENT

WILLIAM L. LANE

HENDRICKSON
PUBLISHERS
PEABODY, MASSACHUSETTS 01961-3473

HEBREWS: A CALL TO COMMITMENT

Copyright © 1985 by William L. Lane

Hendrickson Publishers, Inc. edition

ISBN: 0-943575-03-6

reprinted from the edition originally titled
Call to Commitment: Responding to the Message of Hebrews

First printing, August 1988

Printed in the United States of America

With gratitude in Christ
To Pastor Ralph Williams
Immanuel Gospel Church, New Britain, Connecticut,
who thirty-three years ago expressed a pastoral
concern for the welfare of a young man that
influenced the direction of his whole life.

He embodied the plaque that hung on the wall of his study:

"When the Lord looks me over
he will not judge me
by the degrees I have earned
or the awards I have won
but by the scars I have incurred."

*Remember your leaders, as those who
spoke the word of God to you. Consider
the outcome of their way of life and
imitate their faith.* Hebrews 13:7

Contents

Foreword

We claim to be people of the Bible. In actual practice we tend to have a few favorite books to which we continue to return. These may include the Psalms, the prophecy of Isaiah, a gospel—perhaps Mark or John—and one or more of Paul's letters. Our exposure to the remainder of the biblical legacy which has been preserved for us is rather limited. What we mean when we refer to the Bible is less than the full heritage.

In my own experience I have frequently neglected certain books of the Bible. This fact, frankly, is surprising because I claim to be *a person under authority*. I stand under the authority of the lordship of Jesus Christ and under the authority of the word of God. Perhaps that is where you stand as well. In the light of that fact I am surprised at our reluctance and slowness to claim all of the Bible for ourselves. A rich legacy has been left to us in the Scripture. Yet in our approach to the reading of the Bible there are many portions of God's word that we have neglected.

The book of Hebrews is one of those portions. When talking with people about their favorite books of the Bible, on only one occasion did a woman say to me, "When I was a young woman I read Hebrews again and again. And whenever someone asked me about my favorite book of the Bible I always spoke of Hebrews." But then she added, "But I can't really remember what it was in Hebrews that so deeply impressed me."

For the past six years I have been working on the preparation of a major commentary on Hebrews. When I share this fact with others, the response is almost invariably the same: "Hebrews is a very difficult book." I interpret the response to mean: "I've heard that Hebrews is a difficult book. My own exposure to the book is rather limited."

There is a widespread conviction that Hebrews is a particularly difficult book. It tends to be neglected in preaching. Only rarely is a study of Hebrews included among the courses offered in seminaries. When we gather together for Bible study we seldom concentrate on Hebrews. The book is frequently omitted in personal, devotional reading of the Bible.

Hebrews is a difficult book. But I am convinced that it is one of the special gifts of God to his Church. It is a gift to be appreciated especially when God's people find themselves prone to discouragement or distraction from any cause. The studies presented here seek to unwrap that gift and to exhibit its worth and splendor.

These studies were prepared originally as a gift to the community of Bowling Green, Kentucky in commemoration of the Year of the Bible. They were commissioned by the pastor and people of the First Free Methodist Church (now the Fountain Square Church), to whom they were presented as an eleven-week series of messages which were televised during the week to the larger community through a cable network. They are offered here in a revised format in response to the encouragement of those who first heard them as delivered.

In revising the presentations for publication I have sought to prepare a book which could serve as a teaching manual for study groups or individuals. Certain features of the format reflect this goal:

(1) frequent citation of the text in order to foster engagement with the detail of the statement in Hebrews;

(2) free use of first and second personal pronouns in order to encourage identification with the concerns of the writer and with those of the community of men and women whom he addressed;

(3) highlighting by italics in order to indicate significant terms, observations, and conclusions;

(4) repetition of key observations, and sometimes of the argument, as a deliberate teaching device;

(5) a summary of the previous chapter by way of review and of emphasizing significant points of transition from one section of the document to the next;

(6) inclusion of tables and outlines to demonstrate how the structure of a unit or section serves to advance the communication of the message.

I have sought to express myself with clarity. I have not hesitated to appeal to sources extraneous to Hebrews in order to illustrate the significance of Hebrews.

The translation of the text of Hebrews is my own. Supporting detail for the translation and the exposition of the text will be found in my forthcoming commentary on Hebrews, which will be released in the Word Biblical Commentary series.

May God, who in the past spoke to the fathers through the prophets but who in this present time speaks his definitive word through his Son, breathe life into these words that you may better hear his voice today.

> William L. Lane
> February 23, 1985
> *The Feast of Polycarp of Smyrna, Martyr*

HEBREWS

A CALL TO COMMITMENT

I

A Sermon in Search of a Setting

It is worth asking why Hebrews has been so commonly neglected in the course of preaching, study, and devotional reading of the Bible. A number of factors may have contributed to this neglect.

(1) *Its form seems unusual.* Hebrews is grouped with the letters of the New Testament; we speak of "the letter to the Hebrews" or of "the epistle to the Hebrews." The canonical order of the documents of the New Testament reflects this understanding. The thirteen letters of Paul are followed by Hebrews, then the letter of James, the letters of Peter, of John and of Jude, followed by Revelation, which not only has the form of a letter but contains seven letters to the churches. The placement of Hebrews among the letters leads us to expect that we can turn to this document and find within it what we find in the more familiar letters of Paul: "Paul, an apostle of Christ Jesus by the will of God...to the church of God in Corinth..., grace and peace to you from God our Father and the Lord Jesus Christ."

Yet Hebrews does not possess the form of an ancient letter. The writer fails to identify himself or the group to whom he is writing. There is no opening prayer for grace or peace. There is no declaration of thanksgiving or blessing. The document begins with a majestic sentence celebrating the dignity of the Son of God through whom God has spoken his final word:

In the past God spoke to the fathers at various times and in many ways through the prophets, but in this final age he has spoken to us by his Son, whom he appointed heir of everything, and who yet is the one through whom he created the world. This Son, although the radiance of God's glory and the exact representation of his nature, and although sustaining the universe by his powerful word, yet made purification for sins and then sat down at the right hand of the divine Majesty on high, having been exalted as

far above the angels as the name which he has inherited is superior to theirs
(1:1-4).

This is a magnificent statement. But we have never in the New
Testament read a letter that begins in this manner. Hebrews does
not seem to possess the form of a letter. The distinctiveness of its
form may have deterred us from a serious involvement with Hebrews.

(2) *Its setting in life seems uncertain.* We do not know who
wrote this book or where he was working when he first learned
of a crisis in the life of some of his friends. We know nothing of
the actual circumstances that prompted the composition of this
document. Did the writer receive a letter from one of his friends?
Was he approached by a messenger who arrived unexpectedly,
blurting out the details which moved him to take up his pen? We
simply do not know.

We possess only faint clues concerning the situation of those
whom he addressed. Where did they reside? To what pressures
were they being exposed? How long had they been Christians?
How rich had their experience been when they encountered a crisis of faith?

The evidence to be gathered from the document itself is open
to divergent interpretations. Any reconstruction of the life situation that makes Hebrews intelligible must be put forth tenta-
tively as a working proposal. The task is like piecing together
fragments of a broken mirror scattered upon the floor. When the
reconstruction is completed important pieces may still be miss-
ing, and the reflected image may be distorted. This fact may dis-
courage many persons from reading Hebrews. The document
appears to lack a context in life.

(3) *Its argument seems unfamiliar.* Hebrews speaks of Christ
and of his relationship to the angels in the opening chapter and
then delves heavily into the categories of priesthood and sacrifice. It draws much from Leviticus; unfortunately, Leviticus is
another book of the Bible that we do not read. It speaks of the
provision that God made for an annual Day of Atonement. We
do not think in such terms, and most Christians are hard-pressed
if asked to fix even the calendar date for the observance of this
solemn occasion. It appeals to the experience of Israel in the wilderness and to the conditions for worship during the period of
the tabernacle. It makes reference to the mysterious person of
Melchizedek and to the solemn promise in Psalm 110:4 that God

would establish a priesthood like that of Melchizedek. None of this strikes us as having genuine relevance to our situation. As a result we turn elsewhere in our Bibles for instruction, guidance, and comfort.

Other factors may have encouraged the neglect of Hebrews. It displays a heavy dependence upon the Old Testament. The fact that it does so in the opening chapter may intimidate us. Is it necessary to know a great deal about the Old Testament in order to understand the message of Hebrews? The conviction that we must have a certain competence in the Old Testament in order to penetrate Hebrews makes us uncomfortable, and we put the book aside.

It may be that the sheer length of Hebrews puts us off. We tend to prefer a shorter book like Philippians. A book of that length can be grasped and digested more easily. We appreciate a short gospel like Mark. Hebrews appears to be too long.

What is to be made of that famous passage in chapter 6 which speaks of the impossibility of renewing certain persons to repentance? Does it affirm that Christians can actually fall away from the Lord once they have experienced the grace of God? Hebrews *is* a difficult book, and the result has been neglect. It has frequently been lost to the Church. I am convinced that we have been impoverished by this loss.

What, then, can we say about Hebrews today? Are there facts about Hebrews that make this book more similar to our situation than we realize? Are there factors that will enable us to identify ourselves with the writer and his friends, and which will encourage us to read Hebrews with confidence? I am impressed with a number of considerations that help to bring Hebrews into the realm of our own experience.

(1) *Hebrews is a sermon.* It is not a letter. When we read Hebrews we are exposing ourselves to early Christian preaching. Hebrews opens as we might expect a sermon to begin, with a sharp focus upon God who has spoken in the past and who is speaking at the present time. "In the past God spoke to the fathers at various times and in many ways through the prophets, but in this final age he has spoken to us by his Son" (1:1-2*a*). We should approach Hebrews as we would approach any sermon, with a readiness to hear what a pastor, who is sensitive to God and deeply concerned for his people, has to say.

The impression that Hebrews is a sermon is confirmed by the writer himself. In brief personal remarks added at the end

(13:18-25) he says: "Brothers and sisters, I urge you to bear with the word of exhortation, for I have written to you only briefly" (13:22). He uses the interesting expression "word of exhortation" to describe what he has prepared for his friends. This descriptive phrase occurs elsewhere in the New Testament only in Acts 13:15, where the context is important. Paul and Barnabas are conducting a mission at Antioch of Pisidia in Galatia. They have taken their place in the synagogue on the evening of the Sabbath. At a certain point in the service an invitation is extended to them to address the congregation: "After the reading of the Law and the Prophets, the synagogue rulers sent word to Paul and to Barnabas saying, 'Brothers, if you have a word of exhortation for the people please deliver it now.'" In this context "word of exhortation" is clearly a descriptive term for the sermon following the reading from the Law and the Prophets in the synagogue service. Consequently, when our writer says to the congregation he addressed, "I ask you to listen to the word of exhortation I have prepared for you," he uses the normal designation for a sermon.

The fact that Hebrews is a sermon is an encouragement to me. I have listened to many sermons; a sermon is an aspect of experience with which I am thoroughly familiar. I am particularly interested in a sermon that was prepared under the inspiration of God. I find within myself an eagerness to listen because I am confident that the writer's exhortation will consist of strong encouragement and helpful warning. That is precisely the character of the sermon which the writer of Hebrews prepared for his friends.

This sermon concerns the God who speaks. It is about God who has spoken to his people in the past, and who is speaking to his people in the present time (1:1-2*a*). It is an urgent call for the people of God to listen to the word he has spoken: "We must pay the closest attention, therefore, to what we have heard, so that we do not drift off course" (2:1). The emphasis on listening to the voice of God is sustained throughout Hebrews. For example:

Today, if you hear his voice, do not harden your hearts as you did in the rebellion on the day of testing in the desert, where your fathers put me to the test through distrust, even though they saw my judgments for forty years (3:7-9).

This quotation from Psalm 95:7-9 is developed by the writer as a major theme in the section which follows:

As has just been said: "Today, if you hear his voice, do not harden your hearts as you did in the rebellion"(3:15).

God again appointed a certain day, saying in the Psalter so much later "Today" in the text already quoted: "Today, if you hear his voice, do not harden your hearts" (4:7).

The section introduced with the quotation from Psalm 95 concludes with the writer's sober comment:

For the word of God is living and effective. Sharper than any double-edged sword, it penetrates so as to separate soul and spirit, both joints and marrow, and is able to judge the thoughts and deliberations of the heart. Nothing in creation is hidden from God's sight, but everything is uncovered and exposed to the eyes of the one to whom we must give an account (4:12-13)

The writer calls his friends to listen to the word of God as it has been given to them through the gift of Scripture. God's word is alive. It penetrates. It exposes. It judges the thoughts and attitudes of the heart.

The writer sustains the theme that God is speaking every time he cites Scripture. He likes to use the present tense to emphasize that the word spoken in the past is being spoken once again at the present time. For example:

So then, as the Holy Spirit *is saying* [followed by the quotation of Psalm 95:7-11] (3:7).
So it is when Christ comes into the world he *says* [followed by the quotation of Psalm 40:6-8] (10:5).
And the Holy Spirit also *testifies* to us [followed by the quotation of Jer. 31:33-34] (10:15).

The writer insists that it is imperative to listen to the voice of God *now*. He makes this indelibly clear when he brings his sermon to a point of climax with the warning, "See to it that you do not refuse the one who is speaking" (12:25). The emphasis throughout the sermon is upon God who is speaking to his people at the present time, and in the current situation. When God speaks we must be the children of God who listen, and who ask only to be made wise by the wisdom of God.

Recognizing that Hebrews is a sermon permits important features of the style and structure to receive the attention they deserve. The writer wants to convey the impression that he is present with his friends and is actually delivering the sermon he has prepared for them. He carefully avoids any reference to actions like writing or reading that would emphasize the distance which separates him from the group of friends he is addressing. Instead he stresses the actions of speaking and hearing, which are appropriate to persons engaged in a conversation, and identifies himself with his audience in a direct way:

We must pay the most careful attention, therefore, to *what we have heard*. So that *we* do not drift off course (2:1).
Now it is not to angels that he has subjected the heavenly world to come, about which *we are speaking* (2:5).
We have much to say about this subject, and it is hard to explain intelligibly because you have become *hard of hearing* (5:11).
But even though *we speak* like this, dear friends (6:9).
Now the crowning affirmation to what *we are saying* is this: (8:1).
We cannot speak in detail now about these things (9:5).
And what more shall *I say*? For time would fail me if *I tell* about (11:32).

The preacher assumes a conversational tone in order to diminish the sense of distance which separates him from his audience and which makes writing necessary. By referring to speaking and listening he establishes a sense of presence with his friends. Hebrews was prepared for delivery as a sermon to the congregation.

The literary structure of Hebrews also demonstrates that it is a sermon. The preacher is eager to communicate effectively with his audience. He alternates between the exposition of his theme and practical application of the message he proclaims.

The first thought he develops is that Jesus is superior to the angels (1:5—2:18). His concern with angels was intensely practical. It was broadly accepted in Judaism that the law of God had been delivered to Israel through angels (Acts 7:38, 53; Gal. 3:19). The Jewish Christians to whom he sent his sermon shared this belief (2:2) and found in it a strong reason for respecting the law as the word of God. The exposition of Jesus' superiority to the angels (1:5-14) directly prepares the audience for the pastor's earnest plea not to neglect the message of salvation which was delivered by Jesus (2:1-4). The writer then resumes his exposition (2:5-18).

This pattern, which is sustained throughout Hebrews, is characteristic of a sermon. Alternating with the encouragement provided by the preacher's presentation of the high priestly ministry of the Son of God are a series of warnings addressing the neglect of the message of salvation (2:1-4), the sin of unbelief (3:7—4:11), the denial of Christ (5:11—6:20), the failure to continue in the Christian life (10:19-39), and the refusal of the God who is speaking (12:14-29). The proper way to listen to Hebrews is to recognize that it is an early Christian sermon and to come prepared both for encouragement and warning.

(2) *Hebrews concerns the cost of discipleship.* It addresses a

group of Christians who were wrestling with the cost of commitment to Christ. When we read Hebrews it becomes evident that the sermon was addressed to persons whose world was falling apart. The fact that they were Christians brought no privilege to them. In fact, it appeared to mark them out for a fresh experience of suffering. For them the cost of discipleship was to be measured in terms of the loss of their property, their freedom, and perhaps even of their lives (10:32-34; 12:4).

Hebrews was prepared for a specific local congregation. The writer knows his readers personally and identifies himself with them by using the personal pronouns "we" and "us" He expects soon to revisit them (13:19, 23). At many points he displays a rather intimate knowledge of their past experience.

He knows that they had become Christians when they responded in faith to the preaching of disciples who had heard Jesus of Nazareth (2:3-4). He is alert to their failure to mature as teachers of the truth, although they had been believers for some time and were capable of engaging in a ministry (5:11-14). He is equally aware of their unselfish generosity in meeting the needs of other Christians as an expression of Christian love (6:9-11).

The pastor's friends seemed to have formed a small house-church. The admonition, "And let us keep on caring for one another for the stimulation of love and good works, not discontinuing our meeting together as some people are regularly doing" (10:24-25), indicates that they had become weary with the constant struggle they faced as Christians. They were showing signs of indifference and apathy, and some members of the congregation had stopped attending the called meetings of the assembly.

A common suggestion is that the group of Christians addressed in Hebrews were in Rome or in some location near Rome in southern Italy. In the closing paragraph the writer conveys to his friends the greetings of Italian Christians who are with him (13:24). The most natural way of reading the text is that the writer was currently outside of Italy and that his sermon was prepared for a group of believers in or near Rome.

This proposal finds strong support in an important reference to the cost of discipleship that the writer assigns to the period shortly after the house-church was formed:

Remember those earlier days, after you received the light, when you endured a hard contest with sufferings. Sometimes you were publicly exposed to ridi-

cule, both by insults and persecutions, and on other occasions you showed
solidarity with those who were treated in this way, for in fact you shared the
sufferings of those in prison, and cheerfully accepted the seizure of your
property (10:32-34).

The group had accepted the consequences of their bold faith and
had stood their ground. They had suffered public abuse, imprisonment, and the loss of property.

The description of the sufferings endured is appropriate to the
hardships borne by Jewish Christians who were expelled from
Rome by the emperor Claudius in AD 49. We know of this experience through Suetonius, a Roman writer of the early second century AD who prepared biographies of the Julian emperors. In his
biography of Claudius he mentions an incident of social disturbance in Rome: "There were riots in the Jewish quarter at the instigation of Chrestus. As a result, Claudius expelled the Jews
from Rome" (*Life of the Deified Claudius*, 25.4). "Chrestus" is a
common slave name, meaning "the good one." Suetonius appears
to have thought that an individual of that name was responsible
for the riots. Historians, however, believe that he confused the
facts. His source had mentioned not "Chrestus," but "Christus,"
the Christ, or the Messiah. There were riots in the Jewish quarter
which centered in the Messiah, and as a result Claudius expelled
the Jews from Rome.

Jewish Christians apparently had been evangelizing among the
Jewish quarter. When they affirmed that Jesus of Nazareth was
the Messiah, who had suffered death on the Cross, disputes had
deteriorated to riots. The disturbance of the peace invited police
action, and Claudius banished the synagogue and church leaders
responsible for the commotion. Insult, persecution, and especially the seizure of property are normal under the conditions of
a decree of expulsion. If this reading of the evidence is correct,
the writer prepared his sermon for some of the Jewish Christians
who had shared the expulsion from Rome with Aquila and Priscilla (Acts 18:1-2). They had first-hand experience of the cost of
discipleship.

Now, however, it is about fifteen years later. These Christians
are fifteen years older. When a new crisis emerges, confronting
them with the threat of a fresh experience of suffering, they are
compelled to face the cost of discipleship all over again. The situation now facing the community appears more serious than the
earlier one under Claudius. The pastor's declaration that "in

your struggle against sin you have *not yet* resisted to the point of shedding your blood" (12:4) suggests that martyrdom may become a fact of Christian experience in the immediate future. This sober statement climaxes a section summarizing the experiences of men and women who were faithful to God under the circumstances of torture, flogging, chains, and execution (11:35—12:3). The pastor urges his friends to fix their gaze upon Jesus, who "endured the cross, scorning its shame," so that they will not "grow weary and lose heart" (12:2-3).

The Christians who are addressed in Hebrews were struggling with the cost of discipleship. Sometimes we find ourselves precisely in a similar situation. Whenever I find myself in that place I turn to Hebrews. There I am called to consider the cost of discipleship in the light of Jesus' endurance of the Cross, and to affirm my identification with Jesus Christ.

(3) *Hebrews addresses human frailty.* The writer appreciates the fact that as people we are emotionally fragile. He understands that it is possible to become frightened when we are targeted for arrest and our lives are placed in peril.

The year AD 64 is remembered for the great fire in Rome. For the Christian community, gathering in house-churches throughout the city, this year had begun like any other year. Although Christians were sometimes a topic for pagan gossip, the popular distortions and misrepresentations had not seriously affected the social and civil status of the believers.

All that changed in the aftermath of a devastating fire that threatened to reduce the Eternal City to ash and rubble.

The fire broke out in the congested area around the Great Circus, cluttered with shops and a sprawling slum. Then a shift in the wind lifted the ravaging flames to the adjacent Palatine Hill district, the site of the oldest settlement in Rome where Senators had built their homes among the venerable monuments of past Roman conquests. From there it spread rapidly throughout the city. When after six days it was thought that the fire was under control, it broke out again and raged unchecked for two more weeks. Of the fourteen districts of the city, only four escaped the flames. Three were leveled to the ground.

Nero had been absent from the city and returned only when his own palace was threatened. He responded to the disaster by providing emergency accommodations for the homeless and by ordering the reduction of the price of grain brought in from neighboring towns. Sacrifices were offered to appease the gods.

In the subsequent months he entered into an elaborate program
of urban renewal, clearing debris and erecting buildings, parks
and streets at government expense. But none of these measures
won him any popular support. The people were seething with re-
sentment. They firmly believed that the emperor had ordered the
fire. This suspicion was nurtured by the persistent rumor that
while the city was burning Nero had gone upon his private stage
and celebrated the calamity by singing about the destruction of
ancient Troy by fire.

It was to silence such rumors and to distract attention from
himself that Nero ordered the imperial police to move against the
Christians. "To suppress this rumor," the Roman historian Tacitus wrote, "Nero fabricated scapegoats, and punished with every
refinement the notoriously depraved Christians (as they were
popularly called)" (*Annals of Rome*, 15.44). Known Christians
were arrested and tortured. On the basis of their information
large numbers of others were paraded before Roman magistrates
and condemned to death—not for the crime of arson but because
popular prejudice permitted the humiliation of the Christians.

What must it have been like to belong to a small house-church
at a time when all of the resources of imperial Rome were
marshalled against the Christians? In the climate of uncertainty
created by the emperor's reckless action, Christians fled to the
catacombs. The catacombs, with their miles of narrow under-
ground tunnels and tomb-chambers cut in the soft rock, were regarded as places of sanctuary that might be exempt from police
intrusion.

In the year AD 64 martyrdom became an aspect of the Christian experience in Rome. There were several house-churches in
the city, and the group addressed in Hebrews had not yet been
affected by the emperor's actions. But the threat of arrest and
death was real. The writer, with genuine compassion, reminds
his friends of the result of Christ's solidarity with them:

Since the children share a mortal human nature, he too shared in their humanity so that by his death he might break the power of the one who holds
the power of death (that is, the devil), and liberate those who all their lives
were held in slavery by their fear of death (2:14-15).

The reference to those who were enslaved through their fear of
death is not incidental to this passage.

The writer knew that his friends were frightened. They had experienced the paralyzing reality of the fear of death. In their

fraility they had considered what measures they might take in order to avoid calling attention to themselves. They begin by avoiding contact with outsiders (5:11-14), and in some instances they withdrew from the Christian community altogether (10:25). The public confession of Jesus Christ as the Son of God could cost them their lives, and withdrawal appeared to be an expedient measure. We can empathize with their feelings of fear, for we too can become frightened when our world falls apart, as theirs did.

(4) *Hebrews expresses the concern of a friend.* The writer is a friend with a pastor's heart. He understands their peril and their fears—and he cares. He is also a person who was vitally committed to Jesus Christ. He was concerned that if the Christians were arrested they might accept the Roman terms for release—a public denial of Christ (6:6; 10:29). He remembered the conditions that Jesus had laid down for discipleship (Mark 8:34-38). Jesus had warned that if anyone is ashamed of personal association with him and his words, even though one's life is being threatened, Jesus will be ashamed of that person when he comes as the final Judge. Under what circumstances might a Christian become ashamed of a personal association with Jesus? This might occur if one's life was endangered through association with Christ or with other Christians.

The writer's pastoral concern finds full expression in Hebrews. He writes as a friend to friends. He prepared his sermon with a heart full of compassion because he cares for these men and women. He committed the sermon to writing because the situation was urgent; it could not wait for a later time when he might visit them and strengthen them in person. He wrote to encourage the believers in the face of this new crisis to stand firm in their faith and to warn them of their danger if they remained immature. They would incur the judgment of God if they renounced their Christian commitment (10:29-31, 35-39).

His strongest encouragement was to remind his friends of the character of the Lord who cares for them. He displays Jesus in a fresh way as their champion, who not only identifies himself with them but who has released them from the fear of death (2:10-16). When standing before a Roman magistrate, Christians should fix their eyes on Jesus, the champion and perfecter of faith (12:2). They will not enter the arena alone. They will be supported by the one who shed his blood, but who is now enthroned at the right hand of God (12:2-4).

Jesus is also our great high priest (2:17—3:1; 4:14—5:10). Because he suffered he is able to help those who are called to suffer (2:18). His own experience in being exposed to death enables him to empathize with human weakness (4:14-15). In a moving passage the writer reminds his friends that "during his life on earth Jesus offered both prayers and entreaties with fervent cries and tears to God who was able to save him from death, and he was heard because of his godly fear" (5:7). The answer to his prayers and tears, however, was not deliverance from suffering and death but resurrection (13:20-21).

Jesus has become our great high priest by virtue of his resurrection. The writer stresses that "he has become a high priest forever, like Melchizedek" (6:20). The description of Jesus as a high priest like Melchizedek is the writer's way of presenting Jesus as a royal priest who holds his office permanently because he was raised from the dead (7:1-3, 23-24). He is quick to add, "And so he is able to save absolutely those who approach God through him, because he continually lives in order to intercede for them" (7:25). The presentation of Jesus as our high priest establishes the point that the Lord cares for his people and will strengthen them. This was the message the writer's friends needed to hear.

The writer leaves his friends with a word God has spoken—"I will never leave you nor forsake you"(Deut. 31:6, 8)—and he reminds his friends of the response that assurance makes possible: "So we say with confidence, 'The Lord is my helper; I will not be afraid. What can man do to me?' " (13:5-6). The preacher is a concerned friend, and we do not have to turn away from anyone who is genuinely a friend.

What then can we say about Hebrews today? Hebrews is a sermon that is rooted in real life. It addresses men and women like ourselves who discover that they can be penetrated by circumstances over which they have no control. It is a sensitive response to the emotional fragileness that characterizes each one of us. It throbs with an awareness of struggle as it explores the dimensions of the cost of discipleship. Hebrews is a pastoral response to the sagging faith of frightened men and women at a time when the imperial capital was striving to regain its composure after the devastation of the great fire. It conveys a word from God addressed to the harsh reality of life in an insecure world.

If you have ever felt yourself overwhelmed by that reality, Hebrews is a sermon you cannot afford to neglect.

II

New Revelation
(Hebrews 1:1—2:4)

Hebrews is a sermon prepared in response to a crisis of faith. It addresses men and women *like ourselves*. They appear to have been quite ordinary. They were accustomed to gather regularly, perhaps every day, for worship and sharing. They were a house-church. Undoubtedly they had been sensitive to a certain amount of hostility on the part of family and friends when they left the synagogue and began meeting as Christians. Their acknowledgment that Jesus was the Son of God set them apart from the larger Jewish community with whom they lived. They were aware of the suspicion with which they were regarded by both Jews and pagans because of their Christian beliefs and their distinctive Christian life-style. They may have known that they were objects of gossip in the open market, and on the streets that led to the docks or to the pleasure arcades. All of that they could take in stride.

These circumstances changed drastically when they found Christians designated for arrest and violent death in the aftermath of the great fire of Rome in AD 64. Christians suddenly discovered how fragile they were, and Christian faith appeared to be an insubstantial reality. Identification as a Christian could be a prelude to violence; open acknowledgment that you were a Christian could seal your death-warrant. The approach of a detachment of soldiers became a terrifying prospect. News of an arrest, a brief interrogation, and consignment to a humiliating death became commonplace. Many Christians fled to the catacombs. It was imperative to avoid public attention. Circumstances over which Christians had no control had made their existence marginal and precarious.

The members of this house-church were severely shaken. They had to face painful and disturbing questions. How could God have permitted this to happen? Where was God when Christians were being humiliated at the hands of the government? What was occurring called into question God's ability to do anything about the situation. Christian attitudes toward God became ambivalent. God was their sole defender. But where was he? When the question was posed whether God even cared about what Christians were experiencing, it was possible to become angry with God.

Some of those who had been members of the house-church stopped attending the meetings. Those who remained were confused and frightened. Thus far, they had been spared. They had escaped the net of inquiry which had ensnared others whom they knew to be Christians. But their situation was perilous, and they were discouraged. They were powerless. They may have felt abandoned by God. The cost of discipleship was high—perhaps too high. In the members of the house-church we come face to face with *the reality of faltering faith!*

This was the situation when the remnant of that house-church gathered in order to hear a message prepared by a close friend. It proved to be the sermon we call Hebrews. What they heard was a pastoral response to the sagging faith of frightened men and women struggling to keep their own composure in a tense situation of impending discovery, arrest, and possibly a cruel death as a public spectacle.

How are we to envision the scene as they gather? They are a small group, consisting of the members of a household and some of their close friends. They number, perhaps, no more than 15-20 persons. They crowd into a single room, standing or sitting on the floor, while one of their members reads the sermon aloud. Listen to what they hear: "In the past God spoke to the fathers at various times and in many ways through the prophets, but in this final age he has spoken to us by his Son" (1:1-2*a*). What follows is a carefully developed statement about the exalted status of God's Son and about the significance of the word from God spoken through the Son. *The sermon draws attention to the importance of new revelation through God's Son.*

Let us focus our attention on Hebrews 1:1—2:4, and seek to hear what this initial unit of the sermon meant to those who first listened to it. For it is an important principle of Bible study that what it meant then will provide us with a sound basis for discovering what it means now.

As the writer directs attention to the new revelation through God's Son there is a planned progression in what he says. The first unit consists of three paragraphs:

1:1-4 God spoke his final word through his Son.

1:5-14 God's Son enjoys an exalted status.

2:1-4 Consequently, the word spoken through the Son possesses ultimate significance.

The preacher guides his friends in the consideration of God who spoke his definitive word through his Son, to the contemplation of how serious it is to disregard carelessly the word announced by Jesus.

The opening lines of the sermon (1:1-2*a*) bring the audience face-to-face with *the God who speaks*. The preacher confronts his ambivalent friends, troubled by the apparent silence of God in response to their desparate situation, with the indisputable fact that our God is the God who speaks. He spoke in the distant past through the prophets (1:1); he has spoken in the more recent past through the Son (1:2*a*); and he continues to speak through the witness which has been given as a gift of love to that very community (2:3-4). God is not silent, but vocal. *He has repeatedly taken the initiative to disclose himself because he wants to be known.*

That is the import of the opening phrase of the sermon, which refers to the fact that God spoke to the fathers in the past on many occasions and through a variety of forms. The emphasis falls on the factual truth that God comes again and again into our human experience, disclosing his presence to us, precisely when we had suspected that we were alone in the world, trapped in the prison of our own limited resources. God seizes the initiative and makes himself known. He freely reveals himself. *Revelation is the free disclosure of the Revealer.*

How then may we know God, who exists outside of our human "story"? We may know God by becoming aware of the God who wants to be known, and who freely reveals himself by speaking to the human family. Revelation is God's call—a call which creates our story and makes that story significant—because it opens us to God.

The frightened Christians who gathered to listen to Hebrews needed to know that the living God is the God who speaks. They are not confronted by the silence of God but by the vibrant, awesome reality of God's spoken word!

That fact intrigues me, because our culture is very nervous

about the silence of God. Some of the sharpest expessions of that anxiety are the disturbing films of the Swedish director, Ingmar Bergman. Those films are brilliantly explored by Arthur Gibson in his book, *The Silence of God. Creative Response to the Films of Ingmar Bergman* (New York:Harper & Row, 1969). Gibson is a Christian theologian. He has focused his attention upon the integration of the aesthetic statement with the thematic statement in seven films, in which Bergman relentlessly pursues the theme of the absence of God and the silence of God.

In Bergman's film, *The Seventh Seal*, for example, the God-seeker is Antonius Block, a knight returning from the Crusades. Early in the film he stops at a small wayside chapel and enters the confessional booth. He is not aware of the fact that the one who listens to his confession is actually Death. The ambivalence that the knight feels toward God is evident as he speaks from an anguished heart:

> Knight: Why can't I kill God within me? Why does he live on in this painful and humiliating way, even though I curse him and want to tear him out of my heart? Why, in spite of everything, is he a baffling reality that I can't shake off? Do you hear me?
>
> Death: Yes, I hear you.
>
> Knight: I want knowledge, not faith, not suppositions, but knowledge. I want God to stretch out his hand toward me, reveal himself, speak to me.
>
> Death: But he remains silent.
>
> Knight: I call out to him in the dark, but no one seems to be there.
>
> Death: Perhaps no one is there.
>
> Knight: Then life is an outrageous horror. No one can live in the face of death knowing that all is nothingness.

The knight experiences *a felt absence of God*: "I call out to him in the dark, but no one seems to be there."

That is precisely the way that the men and women of the house-church felt. They ask: "Is God *there*?" The writer of Hebrews answers, "*No* because now he is *here*!" He is dramatically disclosed through the word he has spoken. Moreover, he makes himself vulnerable through the word he has spoken, for he knows that the men and women to whom he speaks can reject him. The God of the Bible is the risking, self-revealing God. It is philosophers who speak about *Deus absconditus*, "the hidden God." The Bible knows nothing about a hidden God but only of men and women who hide, and of God who comes to seek them out and to engage them in a meaningful conversation as he makes himself known to them. This is the God who spoke his word most completely through his Son and who addresses the members of the house-church in Rome in a fresh way as they listen to Hebrews.

In the opening lines of the sermon the preacher compares two phases of revelation, reminding his friends of the fullness of their heritage. A careful parallel is drawn between God's former manner of speaking through the prophets and the utterance of his word through Jesus (1:1-2*a*). The degree of parallelism can be exhibited in a table.

THE OLD REVELATION	THE NEW REVELATION
At various times and in many ways	
God spoke	God has spoken
to the fathers	to us
in the past	in this final age
through the prophets	by his Son

Only one expression descriptive of the old revelation is not taken up and developed in setting forth the distinctive character of the new revelation. It is the adverbial phrase "at various times and in many ways." The omission of this phrase implies that when God spoke his word through the Son he spoke *with finality*. The several phrases can be rearranged to exhibit the preacher's intention:

GOD'S FORMER SPEAKING	GOD'S PRESENT SPEAKING
God spoke	God has spoken
to the fathers	to us
in the past	in this final age
through the prophets	by his Son
incompletely.	[completely/with finality].

Significant pauses characterized God's speaking through the prophets. He has spoken completely only through the Son.

The preacher thus confronts his friends immediately with the God who has intervened in human history with his awesome word addressed to different generations of people. His ultimate word, however, was uttered through one who is distinguished from the earlier series of prophets by reason of the relationship he sustains with God. He is God's Son. As such, he was uniquely qualified to be the one through whom God spoke his final and complete word.

The motive for God's speaking on so many occasions and in so

many ways *was love*. That fact becomes clear when we ask why
did God speak again, and this time definitively, through the incarnate Son? Clearly it was necessary for God and the human
family to be able to speak the same language. God is engaged in a
stunning love affair with the human family. In the person of the
Son, God exposes himself as incarnate to satisfy our need to
grasp him with our senses: to see him, to listen to him, to touch
him.

The depth of the supreme and courageous creative love of God
is displayed when he exposes himself fully to those he has created
in a rendezvous at a cross. That is the consequence of the risk
that is the unavoidable accompaniment of all love that is really
free. That is the startling truth that is brought before the men
and women who listen to this sermon in the house-church—and
that is brought before us—in the awesome fact that God speaks
to us through his Son! Our response can only be one of love or
the cruel rejection of the costly love exhibited through the Son of
God.

The primary theme of the sermon, then, is that God has spoken his final word through the Son. The dominant motif in developing that theme is that Jesus is the Son of God. In the
opening verses of Hebrews (1:1-4) one perspective follows another in rapid succession. The writer *contemplates* Jesus as *the
eternal Son*, who bore in his person the radiance of his own glory
and who is the exact representation of God's own being, through
whom God created the world (1:2a-3a). He *remembers* Jesus as
the incarnate Son, through whom God delivered his definitive
word, who made purification for sins (1:3b). He *kneels* before
Jesus as *the exalted Son* who took his seat in the position of honor
at God's right hand, having been enthroned above the angels
(1:3c-4). Like the alternating patterns of a kaleidoscope as it is
turned in the hand, we are asked to consider Jesus who is the
eternal Son, Jesus who is the incarnate Son, Jesus who is the exalted Son.

The conception is richly orchestrated: individual themes are
readily recognizable, but they merge into one another so skillfully that the consideration of one theme inevitably entails the
consideration of related themes.

This character of the composition can be illustrated by the
description of Jesus as the eternal, pre-existent Son through
whom God created the world, who now sustains everything by
his powerful word (1:2b-3). That manner of describing God's
Son draws on a tradition in the Bible and in older Jewish litera-

ture which makes reference to God's Wisdom, or Divine Wisdom. In this tradition Wisdom is treated as a person who was with God from the beginning. In Proverbs 8:22-31, for example, Wisdom is associated with God in his creative activity as "the craftsman at his side" (Prov. 8:30). This type of representation led later Jewish writers to assign four tasks to Wisdom: (1) the creation of the world; (2) the providential sustaining of the world; (3) the revelation of God's truth; and (4) the reconciliation of persons to God. This manner of speaking was familiar to the members of the house-church from synagogue preaching.

In the opening lines of the sermon the preacher does not say that Jesus is the Wisdom of God. He simply assigns to Jesus the tasks that had been assigned traditionally to Wisdom, namely, the creation of the world, the sustaining of the world through his powerful word, the revelation of God's final word, and the reconciliation of the people to God as he made cleansing for sins. *Jesus is presented in the guise of Wisdom*. The presentation of Jesus as Divine Wisdom, sustaining the universe by his powerful word, underscored his ability to sustain those who could be called upon to bear their witness before a Roman magistrate or a hostile crowd.

This same insight is celebrated in a well-known Negro spiritual:

> He's got the whole world in his hands,
> He's got you and me, brother, in his hands,
> He's got the tiny little baby in his hands,
> He's got the whole wide world in his hands.

That is a perspective richly informed by the insight that Jesus is the Wisdom of God in the opening lines of Hebrews.

There is a related theme. It was after Jesus had made purification for sins that *he sat down at the right hand of God* (1:3c). This is the sole reference to the activity of Jesus during his earthly life in the opening lines of the sermon. Its source is *not* the wisdom tradition of the Old Testament or Judaism but profound reflection on the Incarnation and the Cross. God's boldest meeting with the human family was a supremely incarnational one, and it demanded of him surrender to the Cross. This brief, unelaborated reference to Jesus' accomplishment is slanted in the direction of the later discussion of priesthood and sacrifice in Hebrews. But at this point the writer simply says: the effect of Christ's death is cleansing from sins.

The purification or cleansing of the people from the defilement of sin is a distinctively priestly action. The brief statement in verse 3 anticipates the full elaboration of the writer's argument that we have a great high priest who secured atonement for his people by offering his life to God as an unblemished sacrifice. At this point, however, the writer does *not* say that Jesus is a priest. He simply ascribes to the Son a distinctively priestly action.

The motifs of sonship, wisdom, and priesthood are so skillfully integrated in the opening lines of the sermon that they can be isolated and examined individually only at the risk of disintegrating the writer's orchestrated statement. They are all subdominant themes that are introduced in order to develop the dominant theme of the dignity of God's unique Son.

The dignity of God's Son is confirmed by the proclamation of his enthronement and the announcement of his superiority over the angels (1:3c-4). The statement that the Son is superior to the angels (1:4) flows naturally from the central affirmation that he has been given the seat of honor at God's right hand.

In the Old Testament angels were ascribed a broad role in revelation and in redemptive history. It was commonly understood that the Law had been mediated to Moses, the greatest of the prophets, through angels. That understanding was shared by the preacher and his friends, for at a later point in this section the Mosaic Law is described as "the message declared by angels" (2:2). The assertion that Christ is superior to the angels (1:4) prepares for the demonstration of that superiority in the next paragraph (1:5-14). This demonstration, in turn, is foundational to the thought that *the new revelation through the Son is far superior to the old revelation mediated by the angels* (2:1-4).

In summary, in verse 1 the preacher directed attention to the human mediators of the old revelation—the prophets. In verse 4 he calls attention to the heavenly mediators of the old revelation—the angels. He thus frames what he has to say about God's Son, the mediator of the new revelation, with allusions to the mediators of the older revelation to which his friends had responded with respect and obedience. The frame serves to highlight the central importance of the new revelation through the Son.

In the second paragraph (1:5-14) the preacher brings together a chain of Old Testament passages which demonstrate the superiority of the Son to the angels. His purpose is to lay a firm foundation for the solemn appeal he will make to pay the closest attention to the word spoken through God's Son (2:1-4). The several passages from the Old Tesatment were carefully chosen to correspond to the declarations concerning the Son of God in the opening lines of the sermon. The string of quotations has been arranged to parallel and support the preacher's confession of Jesus as the Son of God.

1: 1-4		1: 5-13	
A	Appointment as royal heir (v. 2b).	A'	Appointment as royal Son and heir (vv. 5-9).
B	Mediator of the creation (v. 2c)	B'	Mediator of the creation (v.10).
C	Eternal nature and pre-existent glory (v. 3a).	C'	Unchanging, eternal nature (vv. 11-12).
D	Exaltation to God's right hand (v. 3c).	D'	Exaltation to God's right hand (v. 13).

The development in 1:5-14 thus documents the superiority of God's Son to the angels in a manner which reinforces the confession of his surpassing dignity in the Church. The correspondence between 1:1-4 and 1:5-14 helps us to see that both passages are confessional in nature.

The comparison between Jesus and the angels considers four points:

(1) his name is greater than theirs:
    he is acclaimed as "my Son" (v. 5);
(2) his dignity is greater than theirs:
    he is worthy of worship (v. 6);
(3) his status is greater than theirs:
    he remains unchanged (vv. 7-12);
(4) his function is greater than theirs:
    he reigns at God's right hand (vv. 13-14).

The extended comparison leads naturally to the conclusion that the message delivered by the Son is greater than the message declared by angels and deserves the closest attention (2:1-4).

The superior name which Jesus received at his exaltation is "my Son" (1:5). Jesus alone enjoys the unique relationship with the Father that finds expression in this designation. The declaration "You are my Son" is a royal formula of recognition which is cited from Psalm 2:7. It validates the Son's right to enthronement and accounts for the command for the angels to acknowledge his worth in verse 6. The reason these words are followed by the declaration "today I have become your Father" is that the "birthday" of a king is the day he ascends to his throne. The quotation from Psalm 2:7 shows that God's own witness is the decisive factor in the enthronement of the Son.

There is a certain degree of unresolved tension in the writer's designation of Jesus as the Son, since that designation can be applied to the eternal Son, or to the incarnate Son, or to the exalted Son. The confession of the dignity of God's Son suggests that although Jesus was the eternal Son of God, he experienced new dimensions of sonship by virtue of his incarnation, his sacrificial death, and his subsequent exaltation. These new dimensions find expression in the legal formula of recognition: "You are my Son."

A related comment may be helpful. In verse 7 the preacher cites Psalm 104:4 from the Greek translation of the Old Testament, which was the Bible that he used regularly. He apparently did not read Hebrew, and so he used an accepted translation of the text, just as we do. The text that he read suggests that angels receive from God their form, their rank, and their task. In Psalm 104:4 he found these words: "who makes his angels winds, his servants flames of fire." This clause provided him with a fresh insight. As those who belong to the created order, angels are subject to God's creative activity and may be transformed into the elements of wind and fire. Their changeable character underscores their inferiority to the Son of God, who stands above the created order and is not subject to change and decay. Angels are subject to constant change; the Son does not change. He remains constant. When the created order grows old and wears out, *the Son will remain*.

That is what the Christians gathered in the house-church needed to know. The word that the Son spoke to them yesterday is the word that he speaks today. And the word that he speaks today is the word that he pledges tomorrow and forever. At the conclusion of the sermon the preacher will hold before his friends the assurance that "Jesus Christ is the same yesterday and today and forever" (13:8). His abiding, unchanging quality lends stability to men and women in a period marked by instability.

One other insight is brought to the attention of the audience by this passage. *The function of the Son is to rule; the function of the angels is to serve*. The concluding quotation of Psalm 110:1 furnishes a climax to the string of quotations. It serves to summarize all that has been said in the previous verses about the dignity of the Son: angels are inferior to the exalted Son; they can never share his position or glory. The writer cites Psalm 110:1 in verse 13 as part of a conversation between God and the Son which the Church on earth overhears. Verse 14 adds that angels clearly have their role in the drama of redemption, but it is not at the Father's right hand. They are appointed to service in the

world. The preacher's friends are, in fact, "those who are to inherit salvation," to whom angels have been commissioned for the
rendering of service (1:14). The implications of this fact are startling.

(1) *Christians are never wholly defenseless in a hostile world.* Angels are an unseen and often unappreciated resource in the life of
the Christian. The arena of their service is a world in which
powers hostile to God seek to disrupt the unfolding purposes of
God. Without the spiritual assistance that God has provided
through angels we could not sustain our commitment to the Son.

(2) *God takes thought for his people in their situation.* Angels
have been sent forth by God. God knows of our need to be pro-
tected from unseen malignant and evil spirits. He has sent his angels to minister to us for this very purpose. The statement in
verse 14 thus reminds us of God's constant thoughtfulness. The
formulation "to *those who are to inherit* salvation" clearly implies
the activity of angels in our lives even prior to the experience of
faith.

Those listening to the reading of Hebrews in the house-church
were called to recognize that angels are sent forth on a mission of
assistance to God's servants who find themselves oppressed and
confused in a hostile world.

The reason for the careful demonstration of the superiority of
the Son to the angels becomes clear in 2:1-4. This paragraph consists of a solemn warning to respect the word of salvation proclaimed by the Lord. When we read this third paragraph it is
easy to remember that we are listening to a sermon. The writer
begins with an imperative: "we must pay the closest attention,
therefore, to what we have heard, so that we do not drift off
course" (2:1). The imperative is followed by a rhetorical question: "How shall we escape if we disregard a salvation as great as
this?" (2:3). These are common features of popular preaching in
the first century. An imperative, followed by a rhetorical question, served to draw an audience into the situation, and encouraged them to apply the imperative to themselves. This pattern
was adopted by the street preachers who travelled from town to
town, speaking in the market place or wherever they could draw
a crowd.

In Hebrews there is a close correspondence in thought between
the imperative in verse 1 and the rhetorical question in verse 3:
the appeal to *pay the closest attention to what has been heard* anticipates the peril of *ignoring the message of salvation proclaimed by*

the Lord. Similarly, the warning about *drifting off course* has in
view the catastrophe envisoned in the question, *how shall we escape*? The writer is very sensitive to the fact that he was forced by
circumstances to reduce his sermon to writing. He wants to use
every device that is available that will enable him to draw his audience into the situation and bring them to a point of positive response to what God has declared through his Son.

The close connection between 1:5-14 and 2:1-4 demonstrates
that the study and use of the Old Testament is for the preacher
not an end in itself. It is a service of love to a congregation that is
being tempted to disregard the seriousness of Christian reality.
The weight of the Old Testament witness is that "we must pay
the closest attention to what we have heard" (2:1).

The interest shown in the Christian message by the men and
women addressed appears to have significantly slackened. The
source of distraction is not specified at this point in the sermon,
but the writer warns his friends that it is possible to "drift off
course." In setting forth the consequences of failing to give the
closest attention to the message received, he selects a vivid metaphor with a nautical background. The image is of a ship whose
anchor no longer grips the sea-bed, which drifts dangerously
past the safe harbor. The people of the Mediterranean world
were able to appreciate such nautical metaphors because they
drew their force from what actually happened. The metaphor of
drifting off course was designed to arrest the attention of the
writer's audience on the seriousness of disregarding the gospel
they had received.

As a means of underscoring his point the preacher draws a
comparison between the old revelation, the word of the law, and
the new revelation, the word of the gospel (2:2-4). The basis of
the comparison is the fact that the message spoken through the
angels demanded accountability: "What was once spoken by
God through angels proved to be valid, and every infringement
and disobedience received the appropriate punishment" (2:2).
The appeal to the normative character of the Mosaic Law suggests that the Christians who attended the house-church continued to maintain emotional and social ties with the larger Jewish
community. It was proper to appreciate the awesome character
of the Law. They needed, however, to sharpen their appreciation
for the solemn import of the message of salvation which they
had received and to solidify their response to it. The revelation
delivered through the Son must be regarded with utmost seriousness.

The writer's attitude toward the role assigned to the angels in verse 2 is positive. Although it is never said explicitly in the Old Testament that the Law was delivered through angels, this was a common conviction in the Jewish community because of the presence of angels at Sinai. Speaking of that memorable event, Moses said that God came "with myriads of his holy ones" (Deut. 33:2). The Greek translation of the text, which was the Bible the pastor read, added these words: "angels were with him at his right hand." Stephen, who also read his Bible in the Greek translation, makes reference to Moses who was "with the angel who spoke to him on Mount Sinai, and received living words to pass on to us" (Acts 7:38). He reminds his listeners that "you have received the law that was put into effect through angels"(Acts 7:53). The same point of view was asserted by Paul, who affirmed that the Law was "ordained by angels through an intermediary [Moses]" (Gal. 3:19). The same perspective is found in the younger contemporary of Paul and Stephen, Josephus, and in the rabbinic literature.

"What was once spoken by God though angels" (2:2), is simply an alternative expression for the word that God spoke through the prophets (1:1). That message proved to be legally valid precisely because it was a word spoken by God. And, the preacher adds, a deliberate rejection of the divine will of God expressed in the Law received an appropriate redress: "every infringement and disobedience received the appropriate punishment" (2:2b). The term "disobedience" implies an unwillingness to listen to the voice of God. This was the precise disposition that the men and women of the house-church were beginning to display toward the gospel message they had received. It was this fact that stirred the writer's deep concern for his friends.

That is why he directs their attention from the law to the message of salvation they had received (2:3-4). The decision to ignore the message of salvation entails catastrophic consequences: "how shall we escape if we disregard a salvation as great as this?" (2:3a).

"Salvation" is a word with which we are familiar. It should always be remembered that it is a metaphor which speaks of the rescuing of the people by God. It also connotes a new quality of life; the word can be translated "health" or "wholeness." It refers to the new dimensions of personal relationship that are experienced by those who come to know the God who speaks. This is why the writer asks, "how shall we escape if we disregard a salvation as great as this?" Salvation implies a personal relationship with the personal God.

The term "neglect" suggests a careless attitude, a lack of concern, a disregard for the gift of God. Both the old and new people of God were heirs to revelation. But the demonstration that the Son, through whom the new revelation came, was far superior to the prophets and far superior to the angels, proves that the word which he brought was of far greater consequence. The greater degree of privilege enjoyed by the new people of God entails a greater degree of responsibility and, consequently, of peril if that privilege is callously disregarded. The question, "how shall we escape?" is rhetorical and implies that *no escape is possible*.

The final words of this unit focus on the line of tradition that stands behind the message which the preacher's audience had received. That tradition began with the activity of the Lord himself, who announced the word of salvation. It was "guaranteed to us" by accredited witnesses who heard him. The integrity of the word they proclaimed was endorsed by God through "signs and wonders and many kinds of miracles and by distribution of the gifts of the Holy Spirit" (2:4). God is presented as the Confirmer, who made himself known not only through the word of preaching but through acts of power as well. The supporting evidence that the message of the gospel is the new revelation through the Son is the experience of power in the lives of those who responded to the message in faith.

The confirming tokens, which we describe as the charismatic gifts, were actually an expression of God's love for the human family. They consisted of "signs" that point to the gracious activity of God, of "wonders" that cause us to stand back in amazement, knowing that we are in the presence of God, of "miracles" that call forth the acknowledgment that we could not accomplish these acts through our own resources, and of "gifts of the Holy Spirit" given to us in accordance with God's sovereign will. All of these are evidences of God's love. The supporting testimony was grounded in the will of the God who cares for his people.

The purpose of this confirmation of the Christian message is the validation that God has spoken definitively in Jesus Christ. In the face of such evidence, unbelief and carelessness can only be regarded as the expression of an utterly incomprehensible hardness of heart.

The third paragraph of the sermon (2:1-4) demonstrates the depth of the pastoral concern of the preacher. His fundamental assumption is this: *the character of the messenger provides the test of the importance and finality of his message*. The dignity of Jesus as the Son of God demonstrates that the message of salvation, which had been received by the members of the house-church through accredited witnesses and had been endorsed by God, deserves the closest attention. It demands from us the posture of responsible commitment.

What, then, have we learned from this first unit of the sermon? God does not abandon his people. His word is the pledge of his continuing presence. The word announced by his Son is the word to which we must cling. We turn our backs upon its reality to our own peril.

The possession of the gospel, of the apostolic witness, of the evidences of power bestowed by God, are tokens of God's abiding love. They demonstrate his continuing concern to become open before us and to engage us in a dialogue through which we learn that he will never abandon his people.

The preacher confronts his distraught and frightened friends with the realization that God comes before them in a vivid and loving way in the new revelation they have received through the Son. The spoken word of God is the awesome reminder that God is with his people, even when they have an impression of his felt absence.

III

The Shared Situation
(Hebrews 2:5-18)

What do you say to Christians who become over-whelmed with the sense of their own defenselessness in a hostile world? Do you comfort them? How do you reassure them when their strongest impression is *the felt absence of God*? That was the problem faced by the preacher who prepared Hebrews as a message of encouragement to his frightened friends.

The preacher calls attention to the fact that God is not silent but vocal. The living God is the One who speaks. God demonstrated that fact repeatedly in the past when he spoke through the prophets. He then spoke completely and definitively through his Son. He spoke in the awesome fact of the Incarnation, as he accommodated himself to our hunger to be able to grasp him with our senses. *God is not absent but present with his people.*

This is the meaning of the good news announced by the Lord and confirmed to us by those who heard him. God himself endorsed the truth of what had been proclaimed by deeds of power accomplished in the gatherings of Christians. The fact that the word of preaching continues to be authenticated by signs and wonders demonstrates that *God has not abandoned his people*. He is prepared to share their defenselessness. The Cross of Christ is evidence of that fact.

The fact of our Christian existence is conditioned not by the absence of God but by the presence of God. He makes his presence known through his word and through the gifts he bestows upon the Church. The responsibility of the Christian is to pay the closest attention to the message of salvation delivered through God's Son. That message is the ground of the assurance that God cares deeply for the human family and that he gave himself in love to meet human need.

This emphasis is continued in Hebrews 2:5-18, where the preacher directs the attention of his friends to the Son of God who shares our situation. This theme is developed in three paragraphs. In the first paragraph (2:5-9) the preacher comments on God's intention for the human family, and demonstrates that this intention will be achieved through Jesus. In the following two paragraphs he considers the work of Christ, first from the perspective that Christ is our champion (2:10-16) and then from the perspective that Christ is our priest (2:17-18).

The central fact that the preacher brings before his friends is that the exalted Son of God, who is now enthroned at God's right hand, is *a person who actually shared our situation.* He was fully human. His humanity was exposed to the full range of testing, *just as ours is.* He was made to be *like us.* He fully identified himself with us. For these reasons he is qualified to help us when our faith is severely tested.

The point of departure for the preacher's reflections is Scripture. He read his Bible, and was thoroughly familiar with the detail of the text. In this instance he calls attention to an excerpt from Psalm 8, where he finds the psalmist meditating on God's intention for the man and the woman who were created in God's own image:

> What is man that you take thought for him,
> or the son of man that you should care for him?
> You made him for a little while lower than the angels;
> You crowned him with glory and splendor;
> You put everything in subjection under his feet
> (Heb. 2:6b-8a).

Psalm 8 is an expression of astonishment that God has bestowed so much honor upon humanity. Remembered and cared for by the Lord, created little less than a heavenly being, crowned with glory and splendor, the man and the woman were given the status of creature-king and creature-queen with responsibility for the ordering of the creation under the lordship of God, the Creator-king.

The description in Psalm 8:4-6 corresponds to the divine intention for the human family expressed in Genesis 1:26-28. Created in God's image, man was given a mandate to exercise stewardship over the earth. He was invited to subdue the earth and to put everything in subjection to himself. That goal was frustrated by the rejection of the mandate. The sequel to the creation and commissioning of the man and the woman was human rebellion and the

44   *Call to Commitment*

experience of death as the consequence of sin. But the sense of
wonder expressed by the psalmist indicates that God's original
intention for the human family had not been forgotten. The celebration of the divine intention in Psalm 8 kept alive the hope that
the mandate given to the human family at the time of creation
would be fulfilled, perhaps in the world to come.

When the preacher interacts with the text of Psalm 8, he shows
no interest in the initial lines: "What is man that you take
thought for him, or the son of man that you should care for
him." His interest was confined to the lines quoted in verses 6-7,
where he found an important clue to the interpretation of the
psalm. He was particularly struck by the statement, "You put
everything in subjection under his feet" (v. 8*a*). He takes up this
theme in verse 8*b* and underscores its absolute character by using
a double negative: "Now in putting everything in subjection to
him, he left *nothing* that was *not* under his control." The force of
the double negative is to emphasize the collective expression
"everything" in the citation from Psalm 8:6, "You put *everything*
in subjection under his feet."

The extravagance of that statement is mocked, of course, by
human experience. The pastor immediately adds, "But in fact we
do not yet see everything subject to his control" (v. 8*c*). The tem-
poral expression "not yet" is of crucial significance, for it indicates that the writer found in the quotation from Psalm 8 a
prophecy that eventually will be fulfilled. He regards the words
"You put everything in subjection under his feet" as a legal decree; its realization, however, is yet deferred. That circumstance
provided the preacher with an important clue concerning the
meaning of Psalm 8. *The fact that the decree has not yet been realized indicates that the promised subjection of everything has reference not to man in general but to Jesus, whom God has appointed
"heir of everything"* (Heb. 1:2).

This understanding is made explicit in verse 9, when the
preacher interprets the lines from Psalm 8 in terms of Jesus' experience. The psalmist's statement describes two phases in the life
of the Lord. The line cited in verse 7, "You made him for a little
while lower than the angels," concerns Jesus' temporary abasement. The line, "You crowned him with glory and honor," refers
to his subsequent exaltation and glorification. In fact, the three
lines cited in verses 7-8*a* combine to form a confession of faith
which celebrates three successive moments in the drama of redemption; namely the incarnation (v. 7*a*), the exaltation (v. 7*b*),
and the final victory, when everything will be in subjection to

Jesus Christ (v. 8a). The first moment reflects on the past (the incarnation), the second on the present (the exaltation), and the third looks to the future (the final victory). The preacher read Psalm 8 as a confession of the dignity of Jesus.

On the basis of this insight a number of conclusions can be drawn from verse 9.

(1) *In the person of Jesus we see displayed the actual character of our human vocation.* What does it mean to be fully human? Jesus satisfies God's design for the human family, as set forth in Psalm 8. He shows us what God has always intended for the whole human family. He is the man in whom we see restored the primal glory and authority which God bestowed on man. His experience of humiliation and exaltation guarantees that the absolute subjection of everything envisioned by the psalmist will yet be achieved.

(2) *The fact that Jesus was for a little while made lower than the angels does not call into question his superiority to the angels.* The humiliation to which he submitted was only temporary. It endured only "for a brief while" and has already been exchanged for exaltation glory. It was necessary for him to be made lower than the angels in order to accomplish our redemption.

(3) *For the first time in the sermon the writer introduces the proper name, Jesus.* That is appropriate, because the preacher is focusing upon the humanity and death of the Son of God. What is striking is that he assigns to the name a deferred position in the sentence: "We see the one who for a little while was made lower than the angels—Jesus—so that by the grace of God he might taste death for everyone." We may paraphrase the statement to bring out its force: "we see the one who for a little while was made lower than the angels—I mean Jesus—dealing triumphantly with death on our behalf!" The unusual word order is calculated to arrest our attention. It conveys an element of surprise as well as emphasis.

(4) *The purpose of Jesus' sharing in the human condition was that he might experience death for others.* His full humanity and exposure to death was the condition for the achievement of redemption. The phrase "to taste death" is a Semitic expression which captures vividly the reality of the violent death on the cross which Jesus endured for others. He did this "by the grace of God." God graciously addresses our failure to achieve the destiny he marked out for us by providing a redeemer through whose death many will be led to share in his glory.

(5) *Jesus has been crowned with glory and splendor because he suf-*

fered death. Whenever the preacher refers to the death of Jesus he uses the verb "to suffer." His "suffering" consisted in death. This is the first explicit reference to the death of Jesus in the sermon. The force of the expression "the suffering of death" is to give the thought special stress. The fact that the crowning with glory and splendor was the direct response to the death Jesus suffered assures us that his death on our behalf fully accomplished God's intention.

In summary, in 2:5-9 the preacher resumes his exposition, and leads his friends to contemplate Jesus in his solidarity with the human family. *The exalted Son of God made the human condition, and especially its liability to death, his own in order to achieve for them the glorious destiny designed by God.* The divine intention is set forth in Psalm 8, where the psalmist looks toward the future. That future is bound up with the person and work of Jesus. His free decision to be made for a brief while "lower than the angels" set in motion a course of events in which abasement and humiliation were the necessary prelude to exaltation. His coronation with glory and splendor provides assurance that the power of sin and death has been broken; consequently, men and women will yet be led to the full enjoyment of the glory God intended for them. In Jesus the members of the house-church are to find the solemn pledge of their own entrance into the glorious destiny intended by God for them. That intention will be realized precisely because Jesus identified himself with us.

The reference to Jesus' death in verse 9 prompts the pastor to reflect on the appropriateness of the incarnation and death of Jesus. His reflection extends from verse 9-18, where he sets forth four purposes of the incarnation:

(1) The Son of God had to share our humanity in order to experience death on behalf of others (v. 9);
(2) The Son of God had to share our humanity in order to bring us to glory (v. 10);
(3) The Son of God had to share our humanity in order to vanquish our adversary, the devil (vv. 14-15);
(4) The Son of God had to share our humanity in order to become a fully qualified high priest (vv. 17-18).

Basic to each of these purposes is the solidarity of the Son of God with the human family. Having examined the first of these purposes, it will be profitable to consider the second, third, and fourth, as set forth by the writer to encourage his friends.

The preacher affirms that it is God's intention to lead many sons and daughters to glory (v. 10). The "glory" to which reference is made is the splendor to which the psalmist referred when he said, "You crowned him with glory and splendor" (Ps. 8:5b). God's intention could be realized only through the incarnation and death of his own Son. That is the assertion of verse 10, which provides a commentary on the final clause of verse 9 and particularly on the statement that Jesus experienced death "by the grace of God." The introductory phrase in verse 10, "it was appropriate to God," qualifies the declaration that Jesus tasted death for others "by the grace of God." When the preacher says, "it was appropriate to God," he reminds his friends that what has transpired in the experience of Jesus was consistent with God's known character and fixed purpose. God's intention for the human family could be achieved in no other way.

The divine intention to lead many persons to the goal God had marked out for them appeared to have been frustrated by human rebellion. It was entirely congruous with God's loving character that he should freely decree that the Son identify himself with the human condition in order to rescue us from the consequences of our rebellion through his own humiliation and death. The sufferings of Jesus were appropriate to the goal to be attained. They were embraced in accordance with God's determination to lead many sons and daughters to glory.

The future glorification of these people is secured by the present glorification enjoyed by Jesus. The term "glory" in verse 10 is equivalent to the word "salvation" that the writer has previously used (1:14; 2:3). The clear redemptive associations of the term become clear when the preacher proceeds to describe Jesus as "the champion" of their salvation: "It was appropriate that God...should make the champion who secured their salvation perfect through suffering" (2:10). The designation of Jesus as "champion" is intriguing.

The descriptive word actually used by the writer carries a broad range of meanings, and this fact is reflected in the variety of translations which have been proposed for this important term: "leader" (*New English Bible*), "pioneer" (*Revised Standard Version*), "author" (*New International Version*).

The meaning of the word in any given sentence can be determined only on the basis of the larger context. It is the development of the paragraph (2:10-16) which indicates that the best

translation of the phrase is "the champion who secured their salvation."

As the passage unfolds, the preacher states that it was God's
intention to bring his people into an experience of holiness: "For
the one who consecrates men and those whom he consecrates are
all of one origin. That is why Jesus does not blush to call them
his brothers" (v. 11). In other words, Jesus stands in solidarity
with the human family who, in turn, stand under the call of God
to be holy.

The writer then cites three passages from the Old Testament
which share the feature of *personal affirmation*. This feature explains why he ascribes these passages to Jesus. Jesus is the one
who strides into the assembly to declare God's name to his brothers and sisters and who lifts his voice in songs of praise to God
when the congregation gathers for worship (v. 12). He is the one
who expresses trust in God as the dominant disposition of his life
(v. 13*a*). He is the one who puts his arms around others and says,
"Here am I and the children whom God has given me" (v.
13*b*).The pastor then begins to clarify this last statement: since
"the children" share a common human nature, he too shared
fully in their humanity (v. 14).

What was the purpose of this shared situation? Jesus shared
our humanity so that by his death he might destroy our Adversary, the devil, who held the power of death:

Since the children share a mortal human nature, he too shared in their humanity, so that by his death he might break the power of the one who holds
the power of death (that is, the devil), and liberate those who all their lives
were held in slavery by their fear of death (vv. 14-15).

Jesus is depicted as the champion who came to the aid of the
oppressed people of God. He identified himself with them as
their representative. He became locked in mortal combat with
the fearsome adversary who held the power of death. He over-
threw the devil in order to release those whom this evil tyrant
had enslaved. Jesus is the champion who secured the deliverance
of his people through the sufferings he endured. The translation
"champion" takes into account not simply verse 10 alone but the
distinctive and fresh presentation of the significance of Christ's
death in the paragraph as a whole.

The statement in verse 10 that it was appropriate for God to
make the champion of their salvation *perfect through suffering*
draws upon a special shade of meaning that the verb "to make

perfect" has in the Pentateuch. The verb is used there to signify the act of consecrating a priest to his office (Exod. 29:9, 29, 33, 35; Lev. 4:5; 8:33; 16:32; 21:10; Num. 3:3). In Exodus 29:33, for example, the verb is clarified by a related verb meaning "to consecrate, or qualify someone for priestly service." The "perfection" of Jesus contemplated in verse 10 implies that God qualified Jesus to come before him in priestly action. He "perfected" Jesus as a priest for his people through his sufferings, which marked the accomplishment of his mission. The expression used in verse 10, "perfect through suffering," thus anticipates the full development of this section, which progresses from the thought that Jesus is the champion of his people (vv. 10-16) to the presentation of Jesus as high priest (vv. 17-18).

The implications of the solidarity Jesus shared with God's people, according to verses 11-13, are developed in the balanced clauses of verses 14-15. The preacher remembered that his friends would be listening to his sermon read aloud. He took great care to arrange his statement so that the clauses stand in relationship to one another. The balance in verses 14-15 can be exhibited in a table:

A	"Since the children	
B	shared a mortal human nature	Parallel
A′	he too likewise	symmetry
B′	shared the same humanity	

C	so that by his death	
D	he might break the power	Concentric
D′	of the one who holds the power	symmetry
C′	of death	

[that is, the devil]

E	and liberate those	
F	who by their fear of death	Concentric
F′	throughout their lives	symmetry
E′	were held in slavery."	

The arrangement of the clauses is designed to make the message clear to those who received it through hearing.

The parallel symmetry emphasizes the resemblance of the Son to those who are "the children." He fully shared our humanity.

The concentric symmetry develops a contrast, first between the Son and the devil, the prince of death, and then between liberation and bondage. The care with which the preacher has arranged these two verses indicates that he wants to achieve the effectiveness of a spoken word, even though distance forced him to commit his sermon to writing.

The purpose for which the eternal Son of God entered human life was to vanquish our adversary. He assumed a mortal human nature "in order that he might nullify" the power of an evil tyrant who possessed the power of death and so rescue those who had been enslaved. *The identification of the tyrant as the devil indicates the depth of the human plight.* The devil gained power over the human race when he seduced the man and the woman to rebel against God. This turn of events allowed the reality of death to enter into the human experience. The fear of death has been a fact of our experience since that time.

It is ironic that the person who was destined to rule over the creation, celebrated in Psalm 8, should find himself in the posture of a slave, paralyzed through the fear of death. Apart from the intervention of God, hopeless subjection to death characterizes earthly existence. An awareness of the reality of death is exhibited in feelings of anxiety. The experience of phobias show that we can become enslaved to the fear of death. This was precisely what had happened to the men and women of the house-church that received Hebrews. The reference to "the fear of death" is the first indication in the sermon of the seriousness of the situation. The crisis these Christians faced was demonic in character.

The primary goal of the incarnation was the Son's participation in death, through which he nullified the devil's ability to enslave the people of God through the fear of death. Jesus' death was the inevitable consequence of his determination to identify himself so completely with his brothers and sisters. There would be no aspect of human experience that he would not share. *But in this instance death was not the consequence of human rebellion. It was an expression of consecration to do the will of God.* For that reason, the devil's ability to wield the power of death was rendered ineffective in relationship to the Christian.

The incarnation was thus the appropriate and necessary means of delivering God's people from the devil's tyranny and the fear of death. The fact of the death of Christ displays the costly character of the grace of God extended to the Church.

Costly grace should call forth from us the response of rich love
for Christ our champion.

The background for this fresh interpretation of Jesus—as the
champion who crushed the tyrant that possessed the power of
death in order to rescue those whom the devil had enslaved—is
found in the pages of the Old Testament. The prophets described
God as the Divine Warrior who armed himself in order to defend
his people who were being humiliated and enslaved (e.g., Isa.
42:13; 59:15-20). This conception draws upon an older practice
of conducting warfare as a contest of champions, as an alternative to the costly commitment of armies in standard combat. Op-
posing commanders would agree in advance to settle the military
issue in accordance with the outcome of a contest between two
or more champions representing the two armies. Combat determined the fate not simply of the champions themselves but of the
people that each represented. The contest between David and
Goliath (1 Sam. 17:1-54) is only the best known account of this
manner of warfare.

Although this practice did not extend beyond the Bronze Age,
the tradition of combat between champions provided the
prophets with a basis for the significant presentation of God as
the champion of Israel. For example,

> Yahweh advances as a champion,
>> as a man accustomed to battle he will stir up his zeal;
> with a shout he will raise the cry of battle
>> and will triumph over his enemies (Isa. 42:13).

The passage that the preacher may have had in mind when he
wrote verses 14-15 is found in Isaiah:

> Can plunder be taken from a champion,
>> or captives rescued from a tyrant?
> This is what the Lord says:
> "Yes, captives will be taken from the champion,
>> and plunder retrieved from the tyrants;
> I will contend with those who contend with you,
>> and your children I will rescue....
> Then all the human family will know
> that I, the Lord,
> am your Savior,
> Your Redeemer, the Champion of Jacob" (Isa. 49:24-26).

This passage seems to offer a model for the depiction of Jesus as
the champion who delivered God's people from an evil tyrant.

Jesus himself on one occasion used the metaphor of a contest between champions to respond to certain biblical scholars who accused him of casting out demons by means of demonic power: "When a strong man, fully armed, guards his own palace, his possessions are safe; but when someone stronger attacks him and overpowers him, he takes away the armor in which the man trusted, and divides up the spoils" (Luke 11:21-22). The preacher develops this strand of the gospel tradition into a significant pastoral response to the crisis which threatened to overwhelm his friends.

The men and women of the house-church were experiencing the paralysis of bondage through the fear of death. They were like the captives of an evil tyrant who possessed the ability to intimidate them. The preacher, therefore, calls attention to Jesus, the Son of God, who shared the human situation in order to become their champion and to secure their release. Through his death, he crushed the antagonist who had the power of death, and so broke the power of the fear of death. *What God promised to do as Israel's redeemer, Jesus has done.* He is the champion of his people. They are not to be afraid even when they face imperial opposition.

The final purpose of the incarnation, as reviewed by the writer, is set forth in verses 17-18: Jesus had to be made like his brothers and sisters so that he might become a merciful and faithful high priest in the service of God. The portrayal of Jesus as champion leads directly into the body of the sermon where Jesus will be presented as our high priest. The concept of champion and high priest share in common two elements which may explain this development.

(1) *The element of representation*: the champion represents the people in battle; the high priest represents the people in their coming before God.

(2) *The element of solidarity*: the champion emerges out of the people; he can represent them only because he is one with them. Similarly, the high priest is chosen from among the people; he can represent them effectively only because he enjoys solidarity with the people. Representation and solidarity with the people are the thoughts which bring together in verses 10-18 the presentation of Jesus as champion and as high priest. This is, of course, the first time in the sermon that the preacher has applied to Jesus the title of office, "high priest." That his ministry was priestly in character was implied as early as the opening lines of the ser-

mon, with the reference to the Son "having made purification for sins" (1:3). But now what had only been implied is made explicit: Jesus is a high priest in the service of God.

In speaking of the necessity of the incarnation, the preacher declared that it was necessary for Jesus to be made like these brothers and sisters of his *in every respect* so that he might become a merciful and faithful high priest in the service of God, in order to provide atonement for the sins of the people (v. 17). In this statement the accent falls on the qualifying phrase, "in every respect." That phrase covers every quality which demonstrates that Jesus shared a fully human existence. The pastor implies that Jesus was under a moral obligation to resemble these brothers of his, as one brother resembles another. In this way he stresses the total identification of the incarnate Son with the human situation of his audience.

The reason for the necessity contemplated in verse 17 is explained by two purpose-clauses, which follow in sequence. — (1) *Only by standing with us in human solidarity could the exalted Son of God be qualified to participate in the life of the people as a merciful and faithful high priest.* What this actually entailed is explained in the exposition which immediately follows. The preacher addresses first the quality of faithfulness (3:1—4:14), and then the quality of compassion (4:15—5:10). Both of these qualities led Jesus directly to the Cross.

(2) *Only by standing with us in human solidarity could the exalted Son of God provide atonement for his people.* The second purpose clause is the natural extension of the first, and it describes the activity of the incarnate Son in distinctly priestly terms. The goal of the high priest is the reconciliation of the people to God. It demands the achievement of atonement, the making of propitiation for the sins of the people. The concept of atonement implies sacrifice. In this context the preacher makes it clear that the sacrificial work of Jesus consisted in laying down his life for others (see vv. 10, 14, 18).

The closing statement in this section (v. 18) points up the relevance of the development in verses 10-17 for the community. It is intended to strengthen them in their experience of the temptation to be untrue to God. The incarnation exposed the Son of God to the conflicts and tensions that characterize human life. These tensions were climaxed with the suffering of death on the cross in a final act of obedience to the will of God. It was at that point that his faithfulness to God was put to the ultimate test, and *he proved to be the faithful high priest.* Having been tested in this specific sense, he is able to help those who are currently being exposed to the ordeal of testing. *He thus proves to be a merciful high priest as well.* Jesus' own encounter with a sinful, hostile world and the suffering of death equipped him, as nothing else could have done, to help ordinary sinful, suffering men and women.

The first major division of the sermon is thus brought to a conclusion on the note of pastoral encouragement. *The Son of God shares our situation.* He fully identified himself with the oppressed people of God exposed to testing and humiliation in a hostile and indifferent world.

The exposition in this section invites a series of applications and pointed questions:

(1) God's fixed intention is to lead many sons and daughters to glory. Have you caught the excitement of this provision for your life? Have you ever been gripped by the depth of God's love and caring for you, which prompted this intention? Are you open to being led?

(2) What are the experiences of testing to which you are being exposed? Have you experienced the quietness that is appropriate to the person who is confident that Jesus is at his side?

(3) Are you tyrannized by the fear of death? Are you aware that Jesus has broken the ability of the devil to enslave you through the fear of death?

(4) Have you ever thought of yourself as completely alone in the struggles you face? Have you allowed the flesh and blood reality of Jesus' involvement with the human situation—with your situation—to explode in your consciousness?

The Son of God shares our situation today as fully as he did when this sermon was first prepared.

IV

A Basis for Fidelity
(Hebrews 3:1—4:14)

There are periods in our lives when we feel terribly alone in our situation. There does not seem to be anyone who senses the sharpness of our pain or the depth of our despair. No one comes close enough to share our hurt and to strengthen us with their presence. We feel vulnerable and exposed. Our one desire is to hide because we feel defenseless.

Because every person has felt this way, we can identify with the men and women who received the sermon we call Hebrews. Moreover, we can open ourselves to the truth that *we are never as alone as we felt ourselves to be. The Son of God shares our situation.* He chooses to identify himself with us, and he is unashamed to call us brothers and sisters or to acknowledge us as his "children." He embraces us and shields us from the aloneness that would destroy us more effectively than any combination of external circumstances.

We are not alone. That is the assurance of Hebrews 2:10-18. We have a champion who fights for us—his name is Jesus! We have a high priest who shares our vulnerability. He resembles us, just like one brother resembles another. What set him apart from others who might approach us is that he proved to be both merciful and faithful in the service of God. Moreover, he made atonement for the sins which had separated us from God.

In calling these facts to the fresh attention of his friends, the pastor who wrote Hebrews underscores the importance of the Incarnation. *The incarnation of the Son of God made possible a penetration of our situation.* God knew that this was imperative. The incarnation was an essential means to a necessary end: it permitted the Son of God to share our humanity and to experience

55

death on our behalf. Because he identified himself with us, he arrested the ability of death to humiliate us. No longer are we to be paralyzed by the fear of death. He "tasted" death, but death could not hold him. He is now crowned with glory and splendor. We too shall experience death, but through our identification with him we shall discover that death is unable to hold us. Through Jesus, we also shall experience the glory and splendor God intended for the whole human family.

In the closing statement of 2:10-18 the preacher stresses two aspects of Jesus' experience: (1) his experience of the suffering of death, and (2) his experience of being fully tested in his humanity. What he wanted his friends to understand was that through the suffering of the death on the cross *the incarnate Son of God learned compassion experientially. He became a merciful high priest* in the service of God who is compassionate toward us. In the experience of being fully tested in his humanity, *the incarnate Son of God demonstrated faithfulness to God, and to us. He thus became a faithful high priest in the service of God.* As a merciful and faithful high priest he is able to help those of us who are being exposed to severe testing.

Both of these qualities were relevant to the members of the house-church who felt exposed and alone in a hostile world. The preacher develops the implications of these qualities in inverse order, taking up first the statement that Jesus was a faithful high priest in the service of God (3:1—4:14), and then considering the compassion of Jesus as high priest (4:15—5:10).

In Hebrews 3:1—4:14 the pastor sets forth for his friends a basis for fidelity in the fact that the Son of God is faithful. This unit consists of a short paragraph of exposition (3:1-6a), followed by a long development (3:6b—4:13) and a concluding statement (4:14). The thought can be exhibited in a chart.

3:1—6a   "Consider Jesus...who was faithful to the One who appointed him."
3:6b—4:13   [Will *you* be faithful?]
4:14   A basis for faithfulness.

We are called to consider the faithfulness of Jesus as an incentive to fidelity in our own lives. The basis of our confidence that we are not abandoned to a hostile or indifferent world, and that we can exhibit faithfulness to God in such a world, is the fidelity of our priest.

It is helpful to recall the course of the development which has led up to this particular section of the sermon. The preacher began with a brief paragraph confessing the dignity of the Son of God (1:1-4). He then devoted a longer unit (1:5-14) to a demonstration of the Son's incomparable superiority to the angels. The practical concern which motivates this demonstration is set forth in 2:1-4. There the validity of the word of the law spoken through angels throws into bold relief the superior significance of the word of salvation spoken through the Son.

The exhortation to pay the closest attention to the message of the gospel is followed by a longer unit on the person of Jesus, who brings the divine intention for the whole human family to fulfillment through his ministry as champion and high priest (2:5-18). This, in turn, is followed by a brief unit in which Jesus' superiority to Moses is established (3:1-6). The course of the development can be grasped visually through an outline:

1:1-4   The dignity of the Son [a brief unit].
1:5-14   The Son's superiority to the angels [a longer unit].
2:1-4   The validity of the word of salvation spoken through the Son.
2:5-18   The accomplishment of Jesus [a longer unit].
3:1-6   His superiority to Moses [a brief unit].

The course of this development in 1:1—3:6 enables us to formulate a pressing question. Why was it necessary to demonstrate that Jesus, the incarnate Son of God, was superior to Moses, when it had already been demonstrated that the Son was superior to the angels? Two answers to this question may be offered.

(1) The person of Moses, the mediator of Israel's covenant and worship, was of central importance to the preacher. It must have been a very pressing consideration in the thinking of his friends. Throughout the sermon he contrasts the Mosaic era, the Mosaic covenant, and the Mosaic provisions for worship with the new situation introduced by God through Jesus.

There is a hint of this contrast already in the opening lines of the sermon, when the preacher contrasts the word of God spoken to the fathers through the prophets with the word which he has spoken through his Son, since the greatest of the prophets is Moses. That hint is clarified in 2:1-4, when the reference to the Mosaic law mediated by angels is used to reinforce the ultimate significance of the salvation proclaimed by the Lord and by those who heard him.

As the sermon unfolds the preacher will provide an extended

comparison between the provisions for access to God in the Mosaic era and in Christian worship. *There is a studied parallel between Moses as the mediator of the old form of worship and Jesus as the mediator of the new.* By calling attention to Moses and to the wilderness generation to which he gave leadership the writer is able to emphasize Jesus as the mediator of the new covenant and to clarify the character of Christian life. For this reason Moses and Jesus are yoked together throughout the sermon.

(2) In 1:1—2:18 the preacher has emphasized that Jesus is the transcendent Son of God, the mediator of God's final word. *The authority claimed for the Son invited comparison with the unique authority of Moses.* Moses was the man with whom God had spoken more intimately and directly than with an ordinary prophet. The classic passage for demonstrating this fact is God's own witness in Numbers 12:6-8:

> When a prophet of the Lord is among you,
> I reveal myself to him in visions,
> I speak to him in dreams.
> But this is not true of my servant Moses;
> he is faithful in all my house.
> With him I speak face to face,
> clearly and not in riddles;
> he sees the form of the Lord.

The preacher alludes to this text and specifically to Numbers 12:7 in this paragraph (3:2, 5).

In some strands of the later Jewish tradition the testimony to Moses' faithfulness in Numbers 12:7 was used to prove that Moses had been granted a higher rank and privilege than the ministering angels. One early tradition cites the passage: "If you have a prophet of the Lord, in a vision I will be known to him and in a dream I will speak to him. . . . Not thus have I dealt with my servant Moses, but in all my house he is trusted." The declaration "in all my house he is trusted" is given a striking commentary: "Another interpretation: *In all my house he is trusted*: more than the ministering angels and the sanctuary *he is trusted*" (*Siphre Zuta Beha'alothka* 12:68 [Horowitz, 275-76]). According to this tradition, Moses is honored more than the ministering angels or the sanctuary where God is worshiped!

If this tradition was current and familiar to the writer's friends through synagogue preaching, it clarifies the structure of his own sermon, where the Son is compared first to the angels (1:1—

2:16), and then to Moses, their superior (3:1-6). Although Jesus
had been shown superior to the angels, it was still necessary to
demonstrate that he was superior to Moses, who enjoyed both a
unique authority among the prophets and an exalted status. In
3:1-6 the preacher proves on the basis of Scripture that both Jesus
and Moses were "faithful," but that Jesus has a superior ranking
as Son in comparison with Moses' status as servant.

In an arresting manner the preacher focuses his listeners' attention sharply on Jesus:

For this reason, holy brothers and sisters..., observe that the apostle and
high priest of whom our confession speaks, Jesus, was faithful to the one
who appointed him in his house (3:1-2).

He gathers up what he has said about Jesus by designating him
"the apostle and high priest of whom our confession speaks." The
reference to the "confession" relates the description of Jesus to the
stance of public commitment expressed by these Christians. The
confession signifies a binding expression of obligation and commitment. Public confession is the response of faith to the action
of God in Jesus Christ. The "confession" refers to the central core
of Christian conviction which the writer shared with his friends.
We learn from the final verse of this section (4:14) that the core
was the acknowledgment that Jesus is the Son of God. The reference to the "confession" in 3:1 prepares for the presentation of
Jesus as the exalted Son who presides over God's household in
3:6.

The description of Jesus as "apostle and high priest"sums up
the presentation in 1:1—2:18. He is the one through whom God
proclaimed the definitive word of salvation and made atonement
for the sins of the people. *These combined designations view the accomplishment of Jesus in terms of God's authorization of his word
and work.*

The two-fold description of Jesus as apostle and high priest
may be intended to prepare the listeners for the developed comparison between Jesus and Moses, since both were the commissioned representatives of God. The term "apostle" has in view
this aspect of their respective ministries. Moses was called by
God, appointed by God, and sent by God to represent the deity
at the court of Pharoah in Egypt (cf. Exod. 3:10). Although
Moses is designated a priest only once in the Old Testament (Ps.
99:6), his levitical family background (Exod. 2:1-10), his ministry of the word and privileged vision of God (Exod. 33:12—

34:35; Numb. 12:7-8), and his service at the altar (Exod. 24:4-8)
associate him with priestly functions. The older contemporary of
the preacher, Philo, for example, does not hesitate to describe
Moses as high priest. The designations "apostle and high priest"
could describe Moses or Jesus. That seems to be the background
for understanding 3:1-6.

It is helpful to examine an outline of this passage:

> 3:1-2   Comparison between Jesus and Moses
> 3:3   Jesus superior to Moses
> 3:4-6a   Explanation for this superiority
> 3:6b   Significance of this superiority

Within this structure the writer develops the assertion that Jesus
was faithful to the one who appointed him. We can examine the
statement in terms of the comparison between Moses and Jesus.

MOSES	JESUS
Faithful to God (v. 2b).	Faithful to God (v. 2a).
Faithful as a servant (v. 5).	Faithful as a Son (v. 6a).
A servant *in* God's house (v. 5a).	A Son *over* God's house (v. 6b).

Conclusion: We are his house if we prove faithful (v. 6b).

The argument turns on the distinction between a servant and
the Son, and on the difference between service *in* the house of
God and the appointment to preside *over* the house of God.

The basis of the argument is the conviction that in the ministry
of Jesus we may recognize the fulfillment of ancient promises
concerning a faithful agent of God. The preacher brings together
two prophetic oracles from the Old Testament. The first was an
oracle of God delivered through the elderly priest, Eli: "I will
raise up for myself a *faithful* priest....and I will build him a faithful house" (1 Sam. 2:35). The second oracle was delivered
through the prophet Nathan. God said in reference to a descen-
dant of David: "I will be his father, and he will be my son....I
will set him over my house" (1 Chron. 17:13-14). In the version
of the text read in the synagogue service the oracle was formu-
lated in terms of faithfulness: "I will make him *faithful* among my
people, and in my house (Targum to 1 Chron. 17:14).

This rendering has influenced the translation of the text in the
Bible that the pastor regularly read: "I will make him *faithful* in
my house" (1 Chron. 17:14 LXX). It was the writer's conviction
that these ancient promises have been fulfilled through Jesus'

faithfulness to God, who appointed him to be a *faithful* high priest in the service of God.

The faithfulness of Jesus is the key to the argument in 3:1-6. The preacher readily acknowledges that Moses was faithful as a servant in God's house (vv. 2b, 5). Jesus was also faithful, but he was faithful as the Son appointed to preside over God's house. Faithfulness on the part of a servant is required; faithfulness in a Son is an expression of pure love. The contrast between servant and Son throws into bold relief the superiority of Jesus to Moses.

The basis of this superiority is the appointment of God. The preacher expresses this fact in a tightly constructed statement which takes advantage of concentric symmetry:

A   Jesus has been considered worthy of greater glory than Moses (v. 3a)

B   in the same measure as the builder of a house has greater honor than the house itself (v. 3b)

B'   for every house is built by someone (v. 4a)

A'   but God is the builder of all things (v. 4b).

Because God built the house, Jesus appointed over it

Moses should be honored as one who was faithful in all of God's house, but Jesus deserves greater honor because as the Son he was appointed to preside over God's household (vv. 5-6a).

The preacher then brings his exposition of the Scriptures to bear directly on the situation of his friends: "We are God's household, supposing that we continue to hold firmly to our confidence and the hope of which we boast" (v. 6b). His point is clear: Jesus is faithful to God. We demonstrate that we are the people whom he has been appointed if we also prove to be faithful. This calls for courage in a hostile world. It demands that we hold firmly to our hope of being the people whom Jesus does not blush to call his brothers and sisters (2:11). The preacher says, in short, Jesus was faithful. He asks, *Will you be faithful?*

It is that insistent question that explains the long section of exhortation that follows in 3:7—4:14. The preacher introduces a quotation from Psalm 95:7-11 and then proceeds to bring that quotation into the present experience of his friends. Why did he choose that passage? There are at least four reasons for his choice.

(1) *The passage was thoroughly familiar to his friends.* It served as the call to worship every Sabbath evening when the synagogue community gathered together: "Today, if you hear his

voice, do not harden your hearts" (Ps. 95:7-8). Week after week those who attended the synagogue were called to listen attentively to the voice of God in Scripture with these sober words. They were thoroughly familiar to the members of the house-church through their participation in the synagogue.

(2) *The passage was a sober reminder of the unfaithfulness of the people of God.* The people had experienced God's faithfulness in the exodus and in the wilderness, but they refused to believe in God's word of promise. The focus of Psalm 95:7b-11 is on the faithfulness of God. The substance of the passage can be summarized with the exhortation, "Let us remember the faithfulness of God, and be faithful and attentive when he speaks."

(3) *The passage stresses the importance of listening to the voice of God.* This is an emphasis that the preacher requires in his friends (cf. 2:1, 3-4). There is an urgency to this matter. Psalm 95:7b-11 brings this urgent condition for faithfulness before us in a forceful way: "Today, if you hear his voice, do not harden your hearts."

(4) *The passage underscores the peril of unbelief, and the tragic cost of faithlessness.* The biblical text concludes with the sober pronouncement: "So I declared on oath in my anger, 'They shall never enter my rest' " (Ps. 95:11). The consequence of the refusal to hear God's voice was exclusion from his promised rest.

The biblical quotation from Psalm 95 serves to structure the argument in 3:7-19. The writer begins by citing the primary text, Psalm 95:7b-11 (in vv. 7-11); he then comments directly on the text (in vv. 12-19). The commentary is framed by the use of similar phrases and vocabulary:

3:12 *See to it*, brothers and sisters, that no one among you have an evil heart of *unbelief*.
3:19 So *we see* that they were unable to enter in because of *unbelief*.

The repetition of the key terms in verse 19 serves to round off the section and bring it to a close. In fact, the distinctive term "unbelief," found in verses 12 and 19, occurs nowhere else in the sermon. The preacher wants his friends to find in these verses commentary on the passage cited from Psalm 95.

As the commentary is developed it becomes clear that the preacher interpreted Psalm 95:7b-11 in terms of the account of Israel at Kadesh-Barnea, as recounted in Numbers 13-14. It is striking that in 3:1-6 there was a quotation from Numbers 12:7 (3:5a); now in 3:12-19 there are several allusions to Numbers 13-14. It seems evident that the preacher had been concentrating his devotional reading on the book of Numbers at the time when he prepared this sermon. He found in Numbers a record of the faithfulness of God to Israel in the wilderness.

He knew that the Israelites had travelled from Egypt to Kadesh-Barnea, a point of entrance into Canaan. There was every reason to expect that the exodus from Egypt, the crossing of the Sea of Reeds, and the pilgrimage through the desert would be climaxed by entrance into the promised land. A sense of imminent possession of the land was prompted by the command of God: "The Lord said to Moses, 'Send some men to explore the land of Canaan which I am giving to the Israelites' " (Numb. 13:1-2). The specific task assigned to those who were sent into Canaan was to gather intelligence concerning the land and its population. Is the land good or bad? Are the towns unwalled or fortified? Is the soil fertile or poor? Are there trees on it or not? (Numb. 13:17-20). Those were questions of tactical significance.

After forty days the tribal leaders returned from their mission with abundant evidence of the fruitfulness of the land. Two of the men carried on a pole a single cluster of grapes from the Valley of Eshcol, along with pomegranates and figs (Numb. 13:23-24). The land did flow with milk and honey (Numb. 13:27)! But the intelligence force also reported that it was a land to strike terror in the heart. The people who lived there were firmly entrenched in impregnable cities. There were even giants in the land, the Nephilim and Anakim, and in comparison to them the Israelites "seemed like grasshoppers" (Numb. 13:28-29, 31-33). They concluded that "the land we explored devours those living in it" (Numb. 13:32).

Although this majority report was challenged by Joshua and Caleb, who were convinced that the land could be conquered and that God's presence and promise was the margin of victory which guaranteed possession of the land (Numb.13:30; 14:6-9), a deep spirit of despair settled on the people. They discussed the election of new leadership and returning to Egypt, and even talked about stoning Joshua and Caleb, who had warned them not to rebel against the Lord (Numb. 14:1-10). *The people responded to the Lord with hardness of heart* (Numb. 14:10).

What is hardness of heart? Its character is exposed in the divine response to the clamor of the assembly contemplating violence:

Then the glory of the Lord appeared at the Tent of Meeting to all the Israelites. The Lord said to Moses, "How long will these people treat me with contempt? How long will they refuse to believe in me, in spite of all the
miraculous signs I have performed among them?" (Numb. 14:10*b*-11).

Hardness of heart signifies treating the Lord with contempt; it is
the refusal to believe in the Lord; it is choosing to listen to human
voices of despair rather than listening to the voice of God.

The divine judgment upon the hardness of heart Israel had displayed was severe. Although the Lord forgave the people
(Numb. 14:13-20), he swore that none among those who had
treated him with contempt would ever see the land promised to
the forefathers. Instead, all that they had feared would come to
pass; they would die in the desert (Numb. 14:21-35). This was
the dire consequences of unfaithfulness (Numb. 14:31), sinful-
ness (Numb. 14:34), and wickedness (Numb. 14:35). Too late,
the people acknowledged their hardness of heart (Numb. 14:39-
40), only to exhibit more hardness of heart (Numb. 14:41-45).
Despite Moses' warning that God was no longer with them, in
presumption they sought to enter the land, only to suffer a crush-
ing defeat.

This tragic course of events was called to mind every time the
Jewish people gathered for worship. It is the historical background to the somber warning of Psalm 95:7*b*-11, "Today, if you
hear his voice, do not harden your hearts as you did in the rebellion on the day of testing in the desert."

The preacher wanted to bring this passage into the consciousness of his friends. He begins to do so by casting the formula
of introduction in the present tense: "So, then, as the Holy Spirit
is saying, 'Today, if you hear his voice, do not harden your
hearts'" (vv. 7-8*a*). The stress falls on the fact that the Holy
Spirit is speaking these words to the Church right now.

As the meaning of Psalm 95 is unfolded in 3:12-19, the
preacher underscores the urgency of listening to God's voice. It is
clear that his commentary is based on Numbers 13-14. That
background illumines his sober caution concerning the hardened
heart:

Be careful, brothers and sisters, that no one among you has an evil unbeliev-
ing heart that turns away from the living God. But encourage one another
every day, so long as it is still called "Today," so that no one among you allows himself to be hardened by the delusive attractiveness of sin (vv. 12-13).

He then cites again the crucial portion of the biblical quotation:

"As has just been said: 'Today, if you hear his voice, do not harden your hearts as you did in the rebellion' " (v. 15). The verses which follow demonstrate that the pastor has been reflecting deeply on the incident at Kadesh-Barnea, as recounted in Numbers 13-14. In each of three successive verses (16-18), the initial rhetorical question is framed in terms of Psalm 95, but the succeeding rhetorical question, implying the answer to the initial question, is drawn from Numbers 14:

PSALM 95

v. 16 "For who were they who heard and rebelled?

v. 17 "And with whom was he angry for forty years?

v. 18 "And to whom did he declare by an oath that they would not enter his rest?

NUMBERS 14

Were they not really all those Moses led out of Egypt?"

Was it not with those who sinned, whose bodies fell in the desert?"

Was it not to those who refused to obey?"

In this striking way the preacher brings the tragic sequence of events at Kadesh-Barnea before his friends who were in danger of emulating the hardened heart exhibited by the Israelites.

In applying the ancient story to the church he draws two significant conclusions: (1) we have become partners with Christ, but this presupposes a firm intention to hold to the end the basic position of faith we had at the beginning (v. 14); (2) Israel was unable to enter into God's promised rest because of unbelief (v. 19).

This fresh reading of the familiar call to worship posed important questions for the house-church—and for us—to consider:

(1) Do we possess the hardened heart? Do we display a deeper concern for the counsel of others than we do for the counsel of God?

(2) Does an attitude of unbelief characterize our lives? Does the presence of "giants in the land" cause us to disbelieve the promises of God?

(3) Does our disposition display a quickness to grumble and

complain about our circumstances, as Israel did at Kadesh?

(4) Do we tend to extend a calloused and unappreciative attitude toward one another?

When the Israelites were encamped at Kadesh, the promise was within their grasp. Their trek through the desert was almost over. But at the critical moment they refused to listen to the voice of God. Their refusal to listen exhibits a fundamental refusal to trust God. Their decisive rejection of the divine mandate brings before us *a shocking truth: a participant in the redemption provided by God can choose to disbelieve God. It is possible to display unpardonable indifference to the promise of God.* It was imperative for the men and women who received Hebrews to recognize these facts.

The lamentable account of Israel at Kadesh furnishes the background for the final unit of this section as well, Hebrews 4:1-14. The unit falls into two major paragraphs, each of which is indicated by similar phrases that serve to frame the paragraph. These paragraphs, in turn, lead the listeners to the forceful conclusion of the section in verse 14. The structure of the unit can be exhibited in a table.

First Paragraph (4:1-5).

4:1 "...enter his rest..."

                                     4:3 citation of Ps. 95:11

4:5 "...enter my rest...

Second Paragraph (4:6-11).

4:6 "they did not enter because of their disobedience"

                                       4:7 citation of Ps. 95:7b-8a

4:11 "...to enter...; otherwise you might perish through the same example of disobedience"

Supporting reason (4:12-13).

Forceful conclusion (4:14).

In each of the two paragraphs a citation from Psalm 95 brings the text that is foundational for the entire section before the listeners once again.

The introduction of the unit stresses to the listener that deep privilege entails deep responsibility (4:1-2). The preacher reminds his friends that they have had good news preached to them, just as that Israelite generation who received the good news concerning the land from Joshua and Caleb. But in the case of Israel, the good news received was of no value to them because they did not share the faith of Joshua and Caleb, who had listened to the voice of God.

These comments on the reception of good news and the urgency of responding in faith are directed toward the promise of God. The specific promise of entering God's rest remains open to the believing community (4:1). Here, for the first time in the sermon, the preacher introduces the significant word "promise." That term carries a distinctive emphasis in Hebrews. Elsewhere in the New Testament the word "promise" finds its corresponding term in the concept of fulfillment. What God promised to do through the prophets he has fulfilled by the entrance of Jesus into human history. This pattern is found in the Gospels, in the Letters, and in Revelation as well. In Hebrews, however, a different pattern emerges: promise—promise renewed—with the fulfillment yet deferred. What God promised to do through the prophets he has reaffirmed by the renewal of the word of promise, providing greater assurances that ultimately fulfillment is certain. But in the present time the stance of faith is to live in terms of the promises of God. We can identify with what occurred at Kadesh because, like Israel, we live on the basis of the divine word of promise.

In this context the focus of the promise is entrance into God's rest. What, precisely, does rest imply? Whenever there is reference to the promise of rest in the books of Deuteronomy or Joshua, rest implies the settlement of Canaan. It anticipates rest from the hardships of pilgrimage, from hostility, and from the insecurity and instability of life in the desert through settlement in the land.

In Psalm 95, however, the concept of rest clearly refers to a future reality promised to the people of God. It is in reference to a future rest that the warning is sounded, "Today, if you hear his voice, do not harden your hearts," as did those Israelites who were not permitted to enter into the rest of Canaan. The renewal of the expectation of entering into God's rest in Psalm 95 indicates that the conquest and settlement of Canaan did not exhaust the intention of the promise. God yet has a future rest for his people.

This future perspective determines the preacher's understanding of the promise of rest. Commenting on the renewal of the promise in Psalm 95 he declares: "For if Joshua had given them rest, God would not have spoken of another time later on. Consequently, there remains a Sabbath celebration for the people of God" (4:8-9). In Hebrews the promise of rest is sharply focused on the unending festivity and praise of a Sabbath celebration at the consummation of history.

In support of his conviction concerning an eternal Sabbath celebration the preacher develops a firm theology of rest. The basis of this theology is the recognition that the settlement of the land of Canaan was a type of the rest ultimately to be enjoyed by God's people. The new element introduced in this unit is the reference to God's sabbath rest following the works of creation:"For somewhere he has spoken about the seventh day in this manner, 'And on the seventh day God took rest from all his works' " (4:4). The allusion to Genesis 2:2 is not accidental. Anyone attending a Sabbath evening service in the synagogue would have heard the call to worship from Psalm 95:7b-11, followed immediately by the celebration of God's sabbath rest in Genesis 2:1-3. The writer and his friends were thoroughly familiar with the order of the synagogue service. God's primal rest from his works (v. 4) is *the archetype* of the promised rest, just as the settlement of Canaan under Joshua (v. 8) is *the type*. *The antitype* is the Sabbath celebration following the consummation of history (v. 9).

The rest that is in view, then, is the rest that has been available from the time when God rested from his works. The Sabbath rest of God is the archetype of all rest because it speaks of the completion of work and of deep satisfaction with work (4:10). Israel's rest in the land of Canaan was only a symbolic type of the primal rest of God. That is made clear when Psalm 95 reopens the issue of rest long after the possession of the land was an incontrovertible fact.

Prompted by the Holy Spirit, the preacher invites his friends to conceive of the promised rest of God in terms of the joy with which the gift of the Sabbath is welcomed, as the blessing is recited over the lighting of the Sabbath candles. The delight of that occasion in Jewish homes foreshadows the festive spirit that will mark the advent of the eternal Sabbath. It is the prospect of sharing in the inexpressible joy of that ultimate celebration of the mighty works of God, embracing both creation and redemption, that the preacher holds out to his friends in verse 11: "Let us, therefore make every effort to enter that rest." The alternative is to perish through the same example of disobedience and unbelief which barred the exodus generation from experiencing the rest of God.

The sharp warning in verses 12-13 supplies a supporting reason for diligence. Here the pastor appeals to the character of the word of God as "living and effective." Once more he draws attention to the experience of Israel at Kadesh, when he describes God's word as "sharper than any double-edged sword." God had said to the Israelites, "You shall not enter the land." But the people in essence said to Moses, "We have made a tragic mistake. Let's take up our weapons and enter the land. We are now prepared to believe God" (Numb. 14:39-40). Moses warned them not to go. Entrance into the land now would be an act of presumption, inviting defeat: "You will fall by the sword of the Amalekites and the Canaanites" (Numb. 14:41-43). But they disregarded his warning and entered the high hill country, unaccompanied by Moses or the ark of the covenant. There they fell by the double-edged sword of the Amalekites and the Canaanites (Numb. 14:44-45).

The description of God's word as "sharper than any two-edged sword" in verse 12 is a sober reminder that these Christians were not dealing with Amalekites and Canaanites, but with God. *When we are confronted by God's word we are confronted by God himself.*

In the continuation of the passage the preacher says to his friends, You do not want to risk wrestling with God: "Nothing in creation is hidden from God's sight, but everything is uncovered and exposed to the eyes of the one to whom we must give an account" (4:13). The passage makes good use of a wrestling metaphor. The term translated "exposed" is used elsewhere of a wrestler who has been gripped in a neck-hold and is in danger of being thrown. Philo, for example, speaks of evil men who think it proper to overthrow the good "by using clever and complicated tricks to seize the neck and get their head gripped in a neck-hold, and then by sweeping their legs from under them to hurl them to the ground" (*On Dreams*, 34). The metaphor enables us to visualize the exposed and helpless position of the person who chooses to wrestle with God! The price of reckless unbelief is too high.

The extended review of the unfaithfulness of Israel at Kadesh is calculated to call us to a renewed commitment to faithfulness. The basis for fidelity will be the faithfulness of Jesus, as set forth in 3:1-6. In that paragraph the preacher had demonstrated that in the person of Jesus Christians have a high priest who was faithful to the one who appointed him to his task. That thought is taken up again in the conclusion to the entire section: "Therefore, since we have a great high priest who has gone into heaven, Jesus the Son of God, let us continue to hold fast our confession" (4:14). We have a great high priest who has been faithful to God. He is now in the presence of God, where he acts as our Mediator. His identification with us provides a firm basis for our fidelity, which finds expression when we hold firmly to our confession of Jesus as the Son of God.

It is now possible to survey the progression in the argument in 3:1—4:14. The preacher assures his friends that "we are God's household, supposing that we continue to hold firmly to our confidence and the hope of which we boast" (3:6b). This note of conditional assurance is repeated in the declaration that "we have become partners with Christ, supposing that we hold firmly to the end the basic position we had at the beginning" (3:14). It is sustained in the concluding exhortation, "let us continue to hold fast to our confession" (4:14). In the progressive movement from 3:6b to 3:14 to 4:14 there is a repeated plea for fidelity which finds its basis in the foundational truth that our great high priest is faithful.

In reviewing the section as a whole, the sensitive Christian will be impressed with a number of emphases which emerge from the detail of the text.

(1) *It is imperative to listen to the voice of God in Scripture.* In fact, there is a direct correlation between hearing and obeying. The failure to listen to God's voice leads invariably to disobedience (3:7, 15; 4:7). The correlation between hearing and obeying would have been clearer to the writer and his friends than it is to us, because in the Greek language in which they read their Bible the verb "to obey" is an intensified form of the verb "to hear." Obedience begins with the readiness to listen.

(2) *The pattern of disobedience begins in the heart, the center of the human will.* Hardness of heart is intelligent, planned unbelief. It is possible to determine not to believe God (3:12-13).

(3) *An experience of privileged relationship to God is not a guarantee of blessing.* Hearing a message of good news does not in itself assure the reception of what has been promised. What is required is an active pursuit of the promise and its appropriation by faith (4:1-2).

(4) *The positive response of every single person to the voice of God is of crucial importance.* Throughout this section the preacher ex-

hibits a pastor's heart in the concern expressed lest even one individual should display a hardness of heart and fail to enter God's rest (3:12; 4:1, 11). He could not be satisfied until he was confident that every member of the house-church was actively striving to conduct his life in accordance with God's revealed word (4:11).

(5) *The antidote to unbelief, indecision, and disobedience is exposure to the trenchant judgment of God's living word* (4:12-13). A "living" word is incompatible with stagnation in the life of the Christian.

(6) *The faithfulness of Christ is the only basis for establishing a life which exhibits fidelity to God* (4:14). The integrity with which Christian confession is maintained will be the measure of the faithfulness that is demonstrated in our relationship to God.

V

A Basis for Trust
(Hebrews 4:15—5:10)

Hebrews reminds us of a significant fact: the course of our lives can be plotted in terms of the decisions we have made. Life is a series of decisions. The necessity of making a decision, however, situates us at a crossroad. There is one road to be travelled and other roads to be left behind. We must make a choice. The choice of one option inevitably entails the rejection of other options.

Such times can be confusing and painful. We are fully aware that once a decision has been made, we will have to live with the consequences of that decision. We also know that we have not always made wise or correct decisions. Perhaps that is why we have a tendency to defer a decision until the matter can no longer be ignored. We are uncomfortable with decision-making. Yet to defer indefinitely is to have made a decision. *There is no escape from the call to decision.* That fact was asserted in 3:7—4:13 by the recital of Israel's experience in redemptive history. *We experience life or death in terms of decision.*

This realization was brought forcefully into the experience of the house-church that received Hebrews. The preacher brought his friends before the call to worship sounded in Psalm 95: "To-day, if you hear his voice, do not harden your hearts, as you did in the rebellion on the day of testing in the desert, where your fathers put me to the test through their distrust, even though they saw my judgments for forty years" (Ps. 95:7b-10a). The commentary on that familiar call to worship in 3:12-19 brings us into the vast company of men and women who were called to decision at Kadesh-Barnea. We identify ourselves with them and sense what they feel. This is the scenario.

72

We know the promise of God. We have seen the awesome evidence of his faithfulness to us. But we listen intently to the reports of the tribal leaders who have explored the promised land where God has said that we would have rest.They do not speak about rest. They describe great walled cities with impregnable fortifications. They report that there are giants in the land. Their considered opinion is that we will be devoured by the land. To whom will we listen? Do we listen to the voice of God or to the voices of the men who have actually been there?

On that tragic occasion Israel chose to listen to the voices of men; they displayed contempt for the voice of God. They refused to believe God. And the preacher who prepared Hebrews is quick to point out to his friends that the exodus generation was excluded from entrance into God's promised rest because of their unbelief (3:19).

The preacher brought that painful scene before his friends, making it a present experience for them, because he recognized that their situation corresponded to that of Israel encamped at the border of Canaan. They also had been called by God to live their lives in terms of his promise. In their case the promise had been affirmed through Jesus Christ, and it had been validated by signs, wonders, various miracles, and gifts of the Holy Spirit (2:3-4). Like Israel at Kadesh, the members of the house-church found themselves at a critical point of decision-making. Will they pursue the promise when that pursuit may expose them to public humiliation and martyrdom? Or will they reject the promise and avoid any action or posture that would identify them as Christians?

That decision was examined in the context of fidelity, of faithfulness to God, in 3:1—4:14. There it was demonstrated that the faithfulness of our great high priest provides a firm basis for our own fidelity to God. In 4:15—5:10 that crucial decision is examined in the context of trust, because the question of trust is closely related to the issue of faithfulness. In 3:7—4:13 the preacher reviewed what had happened at Kadesh as an instance of unfaithfulness and disobedience which the church must not emulate. But he could also have considered that critical point of decision in terms of trust and distrust.

Israel decided at Kadesh that they could not trust God. The assembly determined to trust the majority report of the spies who were convinced that the land of Canaan was beyond their grasp rather than the minority report of Joshua and Caleb who said in essence, We can possess it. Their costly decision to disbelieve God was actually a decision not to trust God. *Unbelief is actually distrust*. That appears to explain why the preacher now directs his friends to a firm basis for trust in the fact that the Son of God is compassionate (4:15-5:10). There can be no sustained faithfulness on our part unless we are convinced that we can trust God. *The basis for that trust is the consideration that we have a high priest who is merciful and compassionate in his relationship with us*.

The fact that Jesus is "a merciful high priest in the service of God" (2:17) is demonstrated in 4:15—5:10. He is the high priest worthy of our trust because he is the Son of God who is compassionate. In the second major division of the sermon, then, 3:1—5:10, the preacher considers *the two relationships which are essential* to the exercise of the priestly office, namely, *the relationship to God*, in which Jesus proved to be faithful, and *the relationship to the people*, in which Jesus proved to be compassionate. The notion expressed in the description of Jesus as "merciful" in 2:17 implies a capacity to understand and help those who are dependent upon his ministry.

A smooth transition from the previous section of the sermon is achieved in 4:15. The preacher repeats, with only slight variation, the initial expression found in the conclusion to the prior section:

4:14   "Therefore, since we have a great high priest."
4:15   "For we do not have a high priest who is unable to feel our weaknesses."

The sequence of these statements makes an important point: although Jesus is the exalted Son of God who is now enthroned in the Father's presence (4:15) he is related by experience to a humiliated and suffering community (4:16). *The exalted status of our heavenly high priest does not detract in any way from his ability to empathize with the weariness and defenselessness of the Church in the world*.

In 4:15—5:10 it is the writer's intention to take up a number of themes which were first introduced in 2:17-18:

(1)   Jesus' oneness with the people of God in their trial;
(2)   his priestly compassion exercised in the service of God;
(3)   his experience of testing through the suffering of death;
(4)   his capacity to help those who are being exposed to the ordeal of testing.

The formulation of 4:15-16 recalls the announcement of these themes in 2:17-18 and prepares for the exposition of Jesus' appointment to the high priestly office in 5:1-10.

The orientation of 5:1-10 is determined by the themes enunciated in 4:15-16. The description of the Levitical high priest in 5:1-4 is limited to the note of priestly mercy developed in 4:16. The capacity of the high priest to display compassion results from his own participation in the human situation, a theme anticipated in 4:15. When attention is directed to Christ in 5:5-10 there is a moving description of his solidarity with all those who experience distress. His submission to testing and suffering (5:7-8) was the means by which he was qualified for his priestly office (5:9-10). These emphases flow from 4:15 and give specific content to the assertion that Christ is "one who has been tested in every respect, in quite the same way as we are, only without the result of sin" (4:15). *The purpose of 4:15-16 is to announce the perspectives to be developed in 5:1-10.*

In 4:15 the preacher uses a double negative to assert forcefully that *Jesus identifies himself with those who feel defenseless in their situation*: "For we do *not* have a high priest who is *not* able to feel our weaknesses with us." Stated positively, he is able to feel what we feel. He is able to feel our weaknesses with us because he shared the situation in which we find ourselves. That explains why his high priestly ministry of intercession on our behalf is effective.

The significance of the verb the preacher uses in 4:15 is to share the experience of someone. It must not be understood in a psychological sense, as in the translation, "sympathize with our weaknesses" (*New International Version*). It must be understood in an experiential sense: *our high priest suffers together with the one who is being tested, and brings active help*. When the lash is falling on you, he rushes in so that it falls upon him as well. When you are treated with contempt, he experiences the humiliation that you feel. When you are bruised, he feels the pain. *He is able to feel our weaknesses with us*.

The special shade of meaning in the verb used in 4:15 actually extends beyond the sharing of feelings; it implies more than compassion. It always includes the element of active help. In this context, *the stress falls upon the capacity of the exalted high priest to help those who are helpless*.

This capacity derives from Jesus' participation in full humanity. His own experience of suffering and trials, endured during

the course of his earthly life, equipped him with *empathy*. Consequently, he is able to identify with the covenant people and to
support them in their sufferings and temptations. The preacher
asserts emphatically, "he has been tested *in every respect*, in quite
the same way as we are, only without the result of sin in his
case." He was susceptible to all the temptations that are associated with the weaknesses inherent in human frailty.

An analogy exists between the situation of testing which
Christ experienced and the testing to which the members of the
house-church were being exposed. Were they required to renew
their commitment to God every day? *That was true of him as well!*
Were they asked to trust God in difficult circumstances? *So was
he!* Were they subject to sudden arrest? *That was his experience as
well!* Could they be unjustly condemned to a humiliating death?
*So was he! Jesus was exposed to the full range of human testing. In
this experiential way he acquired the empathy necessary for the discharge of the high priestly ministry of helping.*

His full exposure to testing demonstrated his faithfulness to
God. The outcome of his testing is affirmed in the qualifying
phrase, "only without the result of sin" (4:15c). *His testing was
like our testing. But the result was unlike our experience.* He proved
to be without sin. The qualification "without sin" is a comment
on Jesus' faithfulness to the one who appointed him (3:2). It indicates why his provision of compassionate help is effective. He is
himself the fully obedient one who trusted God, and yet he identifies himself with us. These facts guarantee that we will be able
to endure our situation and obtain the salvation promised to us.

The encouragement offered by 4:15 establishes a context for
the exhortation to prayer in 4:16. The force of the present tense
can be brought out by translating, "let us again and again draw
near to the throne of grace with a bold frankness." The "throne of
grace" is a Semitic expression for the place of God's presence. It
designates the place from which grace flows to the people of
God. The expression is a striking metaphor for God's gracious
presence, and this is how it is interpreted in the *New English
Bible*: "Let us approach the throne of our gracious God."

In speaking of approaching "the throne of grace" the preacher
is drawing upon Israel's experience of worship.The only person
who was permitted to approach the presence of God under the
provisions of the Mosaic covenant was the high priest. Even he
could approach God in the Most Holy Place of the tabernacle
only once a year, on the Day of Atonement, under specified con-

ditions (cf. 9:7). If his ministry proved to be acceptable, the altar of judgment became the place from which grace was dispensed to the people.

What we find in 4:16 is a bold extension of the language of worship. The preacher calls his friends to recognize that the high priestly ministry of Jesus has achieved for the people of the new covenant what Israel never enjoyed, namely, *immediate access to God* and the freedom to draw near to him continually. The members of the house-church may draw near to God in prayer continually with the assurance that they will be graciously received.

The pastor instructs his friends to pray with "bold frankness." The term that he uses has a long history in secular Greek to signify the free and open speech of citizens with one another. It was never, however, used in the context of prayer. It was Greek-speaking Jews who extended the range of the term to include frank speaking with God. Philo, for example, describes Abraham as coming before God with "courage and well-timed frankness" (*Who is the Heir?*, 5). This is precisely the attitude that the preacher encourages in his friends when they speak with God in prayer. Since they have a high priest who empathizes with them they can turn to God with frankness and receive timely help in their distress. *The free right to approach God with bold frankness was granted through the sacrifice of Christ.*

The promise is that God's children will receive mercy accompanied by sustaining *grace*. Mercy and grace are closely allied and essential aspects of God's love. That love is outgoing in providing the protective help that does not arrive too late but at the appropriate time, because the moment of its arrival is left to the judgment of our gracious God. God's loving response to prayerful approach provides a solid basis for trusting him.

The consideration of the oneness of the exalted heavenly high priest with those who are weak in 4:15-16 sets the tone for the exposition of the high priestly office that follows in 5:1-10. The structure of the exposition exhibits a concentric symmetry:

A   The old office of high priest (v. 1).
B   The solidarity of the high priest with the people (vv. 2-3).
C   The humility of the high priest (v. 4).
C' The humility of Christ (vv. 5-6).
B' The solidarity of Christ with the people (vv. 7-8).
A' The new office of high priest (vv. 9-10).

The concentric structure encourages us to recognize that Christ was thoroughly qualified to fulfill the office of high priest.

In the initial verses of this unit (5:1-3) the preacher is concerned with what is true of every high priest (v. 1). He insists on the solidarity of the Levitical high priest with the people he represents. He is selected "from among men" and is appointed "on their behalf" to represent them before God. The preacher's interest in the office of high priest is sharply focused upon his ministry on the solemn Day of Atonement when he entered the Most Holy Place with sacrificial blood "for the purging of sins." This becomes apparent in verse 3, where reference is made to the high priest's obligation to offer sacrifices for his own sins, just as he does for the sins of the people (cf. Lev. 16:6, 11, 15).

The influence of 4:15-16 upon the exposition is particularly evident in verse 2: "He is able to deal gently with those who sin through ignorance and are going astray, since he too is subject to weakness." The thought expressed in verse 2 has no clear parallels in Jewish sources roughly contemporary with Hebrews. Those sources reflect upon the exalted status of the high priest but not upon his gentleness or weakness. The emphasis on the inner disposition of the high priest and his awareness that he too is subject to weakness, which are the distinguishing features of verse 2, is remarkable. It stems from the pastor's reflection on the character of Jesus as high priest in 4:15. *That reflection led him to recognize what God intended priesthood to be.*

The two verses, however, are not parallel. In 4:15 the preacher stresses *the heavenly high priest's relationship to the source of transgression, namely, human weakness.* Jesus is able to feel the weakness of others because he was exposed to testing, even as they are. In 5:2 he stresses *the Levitical high priest's relationship to transgressors.* He is able to extend forebearance and compassion because he knows his own limitations.

The verb used in verse 2 signifies to restrain or moderate your feelings, and so "to deal gently" and considerately with others. The Levitical high priest is aware of his own fraility and sin. That awareness allows him to moderate his own justifiable displeasure and anger toward the sins of the people. His compassion, however, extended only to those who sinned through ignorance or error. Sins that had been committed intentionally resulted in exclusion from the congregation of Israel (Numb. 15:30-31).

In verse 3 the preacher builds on the insights developed in the two previous verses. A reminder of the high priest's oneness with the people in human weakness and need was provided in the continued obligation to make atonement offerings for himself as well as for others in Israel. The high priest remained fallible, and the law provided for an appropriate sacrifice in the event of his sin (Lev. 4:3-12; 9:7). On the Day of Atonement he was required to make atonement for himself, for his immediate household, as well as for the congregation of Israel (Lev. 16:6, 11, 15). Nowhere in the Old Testament nor in contemporary Jewish sources was there expressed the expectation of a high priest who was "without sin."

In stressing that the high priest did not receive his office from the people but from the call of God, just as Aaron did (v. 4), the preacher remains faithful to the point of view developed in 5:1-3. The statement underscores not the grandeur of the office but the humility required of the high priest, who receives his office only through the appointment of God. The humility required of him is consistent with his oneness with the people in their weakness.

The attribute of humility in the Levitical high priest provides the point of transition to the presentation of Christ in 5:5-10:

And no one takes this office of his own accord, but he receives it when called by God, *just as Aaron also was.*
In the same way the Christ did not take for himself the honor of becoming high priest, but he was called by God" (5:4-5).

The humility that characterized Aaron was characteristic of Christ as well, who was called by God to assume the office of high priest.

The pattern for the development of 5:5-10 has been anticipated in 3:1-6. There the point of departure for the comparison between Jesus and Moses was their likeness: both were faithful to God who appointed them (3:1-2). Only then was Jesus' superiority to Moses asserted and demonstrated (3:3-6a). A similar pattern emerges here in the comparison between Aaron and Christ. The preacher stresses first *the continuity* between Aaron and Christ: both were appointed to their office by God. He then implies *discontinuity* and the superiority of Christ to Aaron with the citation of Psalm 110:4 in verse 6, although he defers the interpretation of that important quotation until 7:1-25.

The primary proof that Jesus displayed the humility required of his office, and did not seize for himself the honor of becoming high priest, is provided on the basis of Scripture. The writer brings together two passages from the Psalms which emphasize

God's declarative action. He correctly interprets Psalm 2:7 as *a declaration of appointment*. The same character is evident in the quotation of Psalm 110:4. These two texts declare the decrees in accordance with which Jesus was installed in his office and invested with power.

The effect of bringing these two quotations together in verses 5-6 is to associate the titles "Son" and "priest." "Son" and "priest" are the primary models that the preacher uses to portray Jesus for his friends. In 1:1—4:14 stress is placed on the presentation of Jesus as the Son of God; in 4:15—5:10 the focus shifts to the titles "priest" and "high priest." The citation of Psalm 110:4 in verse 6, in the center of the unit, alerts those who hear this sermon to that shift in emphasis.

One other insight should be drawn from the association of the two psalm passages in verses 5-6. The preacher appears to have understood that the Ascension was the occasion when Jesus was acclaimed as divine Son and priest. The Ascension marked his coronation to the regal office and his consecration to the priestly office.

The primary function of the quotation of Psalm 110:4 in verse 6 is to prove that Jesus was directly called to his office by God. A secondary function is to introduce Psalm 110:4 into the discussion as a testimony about Jesus. No other Christian writer in the first century drew attention to Psalm 110:4, but in Hebrews there are more references to this verse than to any other biblical passage. The text is quoted directly three times (5:6; 7:17, 21); in addition there are eight allusions to the verse in chapters 5, 6, and 7. *Psalm 110:4 supplied the preacher with a biblical basis for the distinctly priestly portrayal of Jesus in Hebrews*. The verse is introduced repeatedly to substantiate the argument that Jesus is a heavenly high priest.

The declaration in verses 7-10 is confessional in character, relating Christ's humiliation and exaltation to the theme of appointment to priesthood. The summary of Jesus' earthly ministry in verse 7 is striking in its formulation. It provides specific content to the assertion that he participated fully in the human condition and that he was fully exposed to testing, just as we are. These moving words express how intensely Jesus entered the human scene, which wrung from him his prayers and earnest entreaties, his fervent cries and tears. The preacher is more sensitive to this dimension in the story of Jesus than any other writer in the New Testament.

Three comments must be made on the formulation of verse 7.

(1) *When the preacher writes that Jesus "offered" both prayers and entreaties, he purposefully uses a technical term for the offering of sacrifice.* He wants his friends to recognize the parallel with the description of the Levitical high priest in verse 1:

5:1 "to offer both gifts and sacrifices for the purging of sins"

5:7 "having offered both prayers and earnest entreaties"

Jesus' prayers were a sacrificial offering. The reference to "prayers and earnest entreaties" in verse 7 is not to particular occasions in Jesus' ministry, such as Gethsemane or Golgotha when he hung on the cross, but to the totality of his high priestly service.

(2) The final clause of verse 7, "and he was heard because of his godly fear," qualifies the immediately preceding clause, "having offered up both prayers and earnest entreaties with fervent cries and tears." *The assurance that "he was heard" is equivalent to saying that Jesus' offering was accepted by God.* The preacher may have recalled that the offering of the high priest on the Day of Atonement was not always acceptable. For that reason he adds the emphatic clause, "he was heard." His offering has been accepted because he proved to be the one who trusted God without reservation. He was fully tested, but he proved to be "without sin." That is why the obligation of the Levitical high priest to offer sacrifice for his own sin (v. 3) was not imposed upon him.

(3) In verse 7 Jesus' passion is described in its entirety as priestly prayer. The preacher's description of Jesus reflects the language of the Psalms, which were interpreted in the light of Jesus' sufferings by the early Christians. In this instance Psalm 116 is particularly in view: "I love the Lord, for he has heard me and listens to my prayer" (Ps. 116:1). As the psalm is developed it describes the experience of being bound with the cords of death, but of being sustained by the Lord (Ps. 116:3-6). *The reference to "cries and tears" describes prayer in a setting of crisis. Jesus prayed with fervent cries and deep emotion.* His prayers were accompanied by a godly fear expressed in the recognition of God's sovereignty and his submission to the divine will.

Although Jesus is the eternal Son of God, he entered into new dimensions of the experience of sonship by virtue of his incarnation and sacrificial death. That is the point that is expressed with a conventional proverb in verse 8. The phrase "he learned from what he suffered" has a long history in Greek literature. The sim-

ilarity in sound between the verbal expression "he learned" and
the expression "he suffered" in Greek invited a play on words.
The proverb was applied frequently to the young and the foolish
who must learn from what they endure. From this perspective,
the application of this conventional proverb to Jesus was very
daring.

The parallels in Greek literature, however, are not the significant factor in the understanding of verse 8. The crucial factor is
that in Hebrews *the verb "to suffer" is used only of the passion of
Jesus, and takes on the nuance of "to die"* (2:9, 10; 13:12). In verse
8 the expression "he suffered [death]" has reference to the unique,
redemptive sufferings of the Son endured in the discharge of his
priestly office. When Jesus accepted God's will for his life and
made that will his own, he honored God as sovereign, and expressed trust in God. He was confident that God would bestow
upon him the office and dignity of high priest promised in Psalm
110:4. From Scripture, and especially from the Psalms, Jesus
learned that his passion was grounded in the saving will of God
and that it could not be severed from his calling.

Consequently, in the statement that Jesus "learned obedience
from what he suffered," the term "obedience" has a very specific
meaning. *It signifies obedience to the call to suffer death in accordance with the revealed will of God.* Jesus freely accepted the suffering of death because Scripture, and the author of Scripture,
God, appointed him to this sacrifice in fulfillment of his office.
The startling assertion of verse 8 is the paradox that *the eternal
Son of God was ordained to suffer death.* Jesus learned experientially through his passion what obedience entails in order to
achieve salvation and to become fully qualified for his office as
eternal high priest.

With great conciseness the preacher refers to Jesus' accomplishment of redemption and his exaltation to the priestly office
in verses 9-10. The phrase "and once made perfect" (v. 9a) announces God's validation of the perfect obedience of Jesus as
priestly representative of the people. Jesus is qualified to come
before God in priestly action because he trusted God and obeyed
him. The acceptance of Jesus' sacrifice asserted in verse 7 with
the emphatic declaration "he was heard" is implied again in verse
9 in the phrase "and once made perfect."

The consequence of this fact is expressed by the main verb of
verse 9: Jesus has become "the source of eternal salvation for all
who obey him." His profound obedience to God, celebrated in

verse 8, demands from the community of faith the response of obedience to him.

The designation of Jesus by God as "a high priest like Melchizedek" (v. 10) follows from the acceptance of his sacrifice. The divine acclamation, "You are a priest forever," confirms Jesus' qualification for his priestly office.

Reviewing this section, it is necessary to emphasize several observations.

(1) *The orientation of this section is intensely practical.* Strong motivation is offered for earnest prayer. The preacher portrays Jesus as engaged in fervent prayer (5:7), and he encourages his friends to draw near continually to the gracious presence of God in prayer. He recognizes the importance of prayer in the rhythm of the Christian life. In order to fulfill their vocation Christians need the quality of experience provided by prayer. Prayer creates a sanctuary when no actual place of sanctuary is available. In the rhythm between exposure to pressure and tired resignation from spiritual conflict, Christians will find in prayer a quality of refreshment that flows from God's invincible mercy and sustaining grace, and they will receive the help that arrives at the right time.

(2) *Although the title "high priest" was introduced in 2:17, the designation is not clarified until 4:15—5:10.* For the first time the preacher establishes the biblical basis for his presentation of Jesus as high priest, and he begins to develop a comparison between the Levitical high priesthood and the unique priesthood of Jesus. In this development Psalm 110:4 will play a dominant role.

(3) *The likeness of Jesus to Aaron is shattered with the citation of Psalm 110:4.* Jesus is "without sin," and he is summoned to be "a priest forever." His priestly task is to create an order of salvation that is valid forever. Moreover, Jesus' offering of himself in sacrifice represents an incomparably deeper identification with men and women in their weaknesses than was ever envisioned in the case of the Levitical high priest.

(4) *The new redemptive relationship between God and the human family inaugurated by Jesus establishes a firm basis for Christian decision.* It demonstrates that we may trust God and persevere in faith and obedience in spite of a hostile or indifferent response from the world. The example of Jesus who places his trust in God (5:7-8) calls forth from men and women of faith a response of obedience: "We will fully trust him."

VI

Peril or Promise
(Hebrews 5:11—6:20)

An examination of language will frequently provide insight into personal feelings about significant matters. The attitude toward *listening* and *obedience* in Hebrews will illustrate this point. The pastor who wrote the sermon we call Hebrews recognized that there was a very close relationship between listening to God's voice and obedience to God. It was ordinary language—in this case, the Greek language—that encouraged that insight. In Greek, as in Hebrew, the verb "to obey" is simply an intensified form of the verb "to hear." The two verbs exhibit the same root form, but the verb "to obey" has been intensified by the addition of a prefix. Everyday language carried the insight that obedience begins with a careful listening to the voice of the one speaking.

That insight offers an interesting perspective from which to approach Hebrews. The sermon begins by calling attention to the God who speaks. In the past he spoke through the prophets, and in this final age he has spoken in his Son (1:1-2*a*). The exalted dignity of the Son accounts for the note of urgency in the call to give the most careful attention *to what we have heard from him* (2:1). The implication is that only when we pay the closest attention to the message we have received will we obey the gospel. Obedience demands attentive listening.

As the sermon is developed the preacher introduces the familiar call to worship from Psalm 95:7, "Today, if you *hear his voice*, do not harden your hearts" (3:7). In other words, Do not close yourself to what you are hearing. Listen with the ear of the heart! The reason for this urgent plea is obvious: Psalm 95 recalls the fact that Israel in the wilderness stopped listening to God. Israel's

refusal to listen to God accounted for the assembly's failure to
obey God at Kadesh. The resultant disobedience was catastrophic for Israel. Behind the formulation of Psalm 95:7-11
stands the insight that *listening and obedience are related aspects of
faith. Refusal to listen and disobedience are related aspects of unbelief.*

The correlation between listening and obedience is pre-sup-
posed in the presentation of Jesus as faithful to the one who appointed him (3:2). His faithfulness consisted in listening to the
voice of the Father. This is affirmed emphatically in the declaration, "Although he was Son, *he learned obedience* through what
he suffered" (5:8). He learned by listening intently to what the
Scriptures had to say concerning his mission. In the statement of
Scripture he heard the voice of God addressing him. The extent
of Jesus' obedience can be measured in terms of his death on the
cross. *He actively obeyed God* when he offered himself for us. He
experienced fully the significance of obedience.

It is as "the Obedient One" that he has been exalted, and "has
become the source of an eternal salvation for those who obey
him" (5:9). The description of the Church as the company of the
obedient is appropriate in the light of the perfect obedience of
Christ, the Lord of the Church.

*It is essential to appreciate the insight that obedience begins with
attentive listening if we are to understand the development of the sermon in 5:11—6:20.* The preacher wants to begin his exposition of
Christ as our high priest and sacrifice. He announced three aspects of this significant theme in 5:9-10:

(1)   the "perfection" or qualification of Jesus for his priestly
       office (v. 9*a*);
(2)   the accomplishment of eternal salvation for those who
       obey him (v. 9*b*);
(3)   the designation of Christ as a high priest "like Melchize-
       dek" (v. 10).

He will develop these three topics in 7:1—10:18. But before he is
able to do so he must address a severe problem in the house-
church. *He knows that his friends are no longer listening to the voice
of God!*

After announcing that Jesus has been "designated by God a
high priest just like Melchizedek" (5:10), the pastor writes: "We
have much to say about this subject, and it is hard to explain in-

telligibly, since you have become *hard of hearing*" (5:11). They
were not listening, and as a result they had become sluggish in
understanding. The development of a "hearing problem" is a
dangerous condition for a company of men and women who
have been called to obey God. The preacher has just asserted that
Jesus has become the source of an eternal salvation *for those who
obey him* (5:9), but this group of Christians has become *hard of
hearing* (5:11). The close proximity of 5:9 and 5:11 underscores
*the importance of listening as prerequisite to the obedience we have
been called to render unto Jesus.*

The correlation between listening and obedience explains why
the preacher prepares his friends for what he has to say about
Jesus as our priest and sacrifice by the strong words of 5:11—
6:20. This section serves to introduce the central division of the
sermon. It is balanced by a later section in which the truths developed in the central division will be applied to the situation of
the congregation. The structure of the development in the central
division can be exhibited in a chart:

Preparation of the congregation 5:11—6:20

A   A high priest like Melchizedek   7:1-28
B   The qualification of Jesus as priest 8:1—9:28
C   The source of eternal salvation   10:1-18

Application to the congregation   10:19-39

The structure of the development underscores the importance of
5:11—6:20 in preparing the house-church for the main body of
the sermon.

The preacher recognized that his friends were reacting to pressures in their situation. They were fearful that they would be recognized as Christians; they could be hunted down and
prosecuted as enemies of the State. They responded by avoiding
contact with outsiders and by keeping silent in public concerning
Jesus Christ. They sought to play the chameleon, blending in
with their surroundings. The preacher addresses this situation in
a forceful manner in 5:11—6:20.

The section consists of two major units. The writer explores
first *the peril of spiritual immaturity* (5:11—6:12). The tone of the
four paragraphs displays an alternation between pessimism and
optimism: 5:11-14 is pessimistic in tone ("You have become hard

of hearing"); 6:1-3 is optimistic ("Let us leave standing the firm
foundation and be carried forward"); 6:4-8 is pessimistic ("It is
impossible..."); 6:9-12 resumes a clear note of optimism ("We
are persuaded of the better option in your case"). The variation
in tone is calculated to engage the attention of the listeners in the
development. In the second unit of the section (6:13-20) *a basis
for steadfastness* is shown to exist in the reliability of God's promise. The pastor thus holds before his friends two options—peril
or promise. *They may expose themselves to extreme peril by closing
their ears to God, or they may find a basis for stability by listening to
the voice of God expressed through oath and promise.*

The initial paragraph, extending from 5:11-14, is sharply pessimistic in tone. Prior to addressing the important themes of Christ
as our priest and sacrifice the preacher must speak solemnly and
candidly to these friends for whom he was so deeply concerned.
The content of the teaching he has to share with them is difficult.
But compounding the difficulty is the fact that his friends have
become "hard of hearing" (5:11).

At this point the writer introduces an interesting term which
could be translated: "you have become *sluggish* in your ears."
This notion seems to be reflected in the translation of the *New International Version*, "You are slow to learn." They were prepared
to learn only at a slug's pace. Slugs, which are essentially snails
without a shell, scarcely move. The use of this vivid metaphori-
cal expression in verse 11 suggests a group of men and women incapable of keeping pace with their situation. Applied to the ears,
it implies that they had become unreceptive; their ears were
closed to the voice of God. *This description indicates a serious erosion of faith and hope within the congregation.*

As a matter of fact, these men and women had been Christians
for a considerable period of time. They had enjoyed a sufficient
depth of exposure to Christian teaching and experience to be
qualified as teachers of the truth. For the preacher quickly qualifies what he has just said in an emphatic way:

In fact, although by this time you ought to be teachers, you need someone to
teach you again the elementary truths of God's revelation; you are at the
stage of needing milk, and not solid food (v. 12).

These Christians had regressed from a level of spiritual maturity
gained over an extended period to the point where they seemed
to need someone to teach them once more the ABCs of Christian
truth. The description of them as "at the stage of needing milk,

and not solid food" is equivalent to saying, "You have become infantile."

It is important to appreciate the character of this language. The preacher has resorted to biting irony. He makes use of sarcasm to shame these men and women into recognizing that they cannot pretend that they have not had a rich exposure to the truth of God over the course of years. In 5:11-12 the preacher makes effective use of a shaming argument to force his friends to recognize that *they are spiritually mature and they must assume the responsibility of mature Christians in a hostile society.*

The character of the argument becomes evident when the preacher contrasts milk with solid food and babies with adults in verses 13-14.

Anyone who lives on a diet of milk is inexperienced with the word of righteousness, for he is an infant; but solid food is for adults, who have their faculties trained by constant use to distinguish between good and evil.

With biting irony, the writer addresses his audience as if they were asking for a milk-diet; he comments caustically in verse 13 that such persons are "inexperienced with the word of righteousness."

The reference to "the word of righteousness" is the clue needed to understanding why the members of the house-church have become hard of hearing and were acting immaturely. The expression is technical and must be interpreted within the context of Hebrews. This sermon summons the Christian community to endurance for God. As the sermon begins to build toward its climax in chapters 10-12 the preacher will speak of the endurance of the martyrs. Although they were stoned, sawn in two, chained, and tortured, they endured for God.

It is interesting, therefore, in the early second century to find Polycarp, the senior pastor of the church at Smyrna, bringing together the distinctive expression of Hebrews 5:13, "the word of righteousness" and the theme of endurance. He writes:

I therefore exhort you *to carry out the word of righteousness* and *to practice endurance to the limit*—an endurance of which you have an object lesson not only in those blessed persons, Ignatius, Zozimus, and Rufus, but also in members of your own community, as well as in Paul himself and the other apostles (*Letter to the Philippians*, 9:1).

Commentators have pointed out that what Ignatius, Zozimus, and Rufus shared in common was the experience of martyrdom.

They were all martyrs, as was Paul. In this context, "to carry out the word of righteousness" and "to practice endurance to the limit" is to hold yourself in readiness for martyrdom. *The expression "the word of righteousness" signifies instruction concerning a willingness to experience martyrdom.*

This distinctive perspective on "the word of righteousness" has its source in Jesus' teaching concerning discipleship, as set forth in Mark 8:34: "If anyone would come after me, he must deny himself and take up his cross, and follow me." To "come after" someone or to "follow" him is to become his disciple. In the context of the reference to self-denial and cross-bearing, Jesus' call to discipleship is a call to martyrdom. "The word of righteousness" became the technical expression in the early Church for the teaching that the Christian must never deny his relationship with Christ, even if he must sacrifice his life (cf. Mark 8:35-38).

This background sheds light in the situation of the congregation addressed in Hebrews and on the argument developed in 5:11-14. The members of the house-church were recoiling from the prospect of martyrdom; they remained paralyzed through the fear of death (cf. 2:15). Their regression to a spiritual immaturity was their response to a life-threatening situation.

In verse 14 the preacher redefines the issue in moral terms: "solid food is for adults who by constant practice have trained themselves to distinguish good and evil." The "adult" is the mature Christian who will recognize the moral claim of God upon his life, even if it exposes him to martyrdom. Those who remain infantile and who refuse to exercise their faculties daily by making decisions in a Christian manner will be unable to exercise the proper moral discrimination between good and evil when they stand before the interrogation of a Roman magistrate. In that case they will be unprepared for the ultimate moral choice between confessing and denying Christ, when the cost of confession and identification with Christ is the loss of one's life. That is the connection between verse 13, with its reference to being "unskilled in the word of righteousness," and verse 14, which describes the mature person as trained by constant practice to disciminate between moral choices.

This house-church that received Hebrews was not spiritually immature in the sense that these men and women lacked theological insight. Their problem was simpler but more serious. They had regressed and had become infantile in the area of making sound Christian decisions. By listening to the voice of their fears, they had stopped listening to the voice of God. The preacher says, "You have become hard of hearing." His concern in addressing this sensitive matter in 5:11-14 was intensely practical.

In 5:11-14 the pastor appears to be pessimistic about his friends, but in 6:1-3 he displays a degree of optimism. He remains optimistic because he knows that the community has been established upon an unshakable foundation. Reminding the assembly of the firm foundation of Christian truth they had received when they first came to faith, he writes: "So then, let us leave standing the elementary Christian teaching, and be carried forward to the goal of spiritual maturity" (6:1). The allusion to "the elementary Christian teaching" refers to the foundational truths reviewed in 6:1b-2. The men and women of the house-church had received catechetical instruction concerning these matters of Christian conviction when they first came to faith. In contrast to those who need to be taught foundational truths, the preacher points to the solid character of the foundation his friends possess. In contrast to those who are immature, he urges his friends to become open once again to the voice of God, and to recognize that God is leading his people to spiritual maturity.

The reason the preacher refuses to review the ABCs of Christian truth with his friends is that he knows they are, in fact, mature. That is why the foundation can be allowed to stand. *The task of the Christian is to remain open to being carried forward by God to a deeper level of maturity.* In 6:1-3 the preacher is saying very simply, You cannot go back in time. You cannot pretend that you do not understand the foundational truths you learned after you became Christians. You cannot act as if you need someone to specify for you what it means to be a Christian in the world. You have to assume responsibility for the level of instruction, knowledge, and experience you already possess.

The writer knew that in the past his friends had boldly identified themselves with Christ in a costly situation of conflict (see 10:32-34). On that occasion they had stood their ground, even accepting joyfully the confiscation of their property. They were firmly convinced that they possessed a better inheritance from God. They had demonstrated maturity in the past. They must stop pretending that they are immature and inexperienced. Hebrews is not a word addressed to those who are immature. *It is a word to the mature.*

This understanding establishes a context for interpreting the severe word of warning addressed to the Church in 6:4-6, where the writer's tone again becomes pessimistic. Hebrews 6:4-6 is a complex sentence. It begins in verse 4 with the word, "Impossible," but the main verb is not supplied until verse 6. At its simplest level, it looks at an impossible situation. The sentence states that "it is impossible...to restore to repentance" certain persons, and the reason for this impossibility is set forth in the clause introduced with the explanatory word "because." The sentence may be translated:

For it is impossible when those who have once-for-all been brought into the light, and who have experienced the gift from heaven, and who have received a share in the Holy Spirit, and who have experienced the goodness of God's word and the power of the coming age, and then have fallen away, to restore them to repentance, because to their loss they are crucifying the Son of God again and exposing him to public shame.

The first step toward a correct interpretation of this difficult sentence is to see it as a whole. Interpretation will be advanced by addressing the passage with a series of questions.

(1) *Who is the group described in reference to this impossible situation?* The group the preacher has in view are described in verses 4-5 in terms of what they have experienced once-for-all. *Once-for-all* they have been brought out of darkness into the light of Christian truth. *Once-for-all* they have experienced the heavenly gift of salvation. *Once-for-all* they have actually shared in the possession of the Holy Spirit. *Once-for-all* they have experienced the goodness of God's word and the reality of the supernatural signs which indicate that the future is breaking into the present. *These traits are true only of Christians.* God's presence and salvation are the undoubted realities of their lives.

(2) *What is the peril to which they are exposed?* The writer warns in verse 6 that they may fall away, an action which is clarified by the "because" clause: "because to their loss they are crucifying the Son of God again and exposing him to public shame." If Christians, who have enjoyed once-for-all the rich experiences described in verses 4-5, were to withdraw from Christ, their own rich experiences would bear witness against them.

(3) *What is the situation in which Christians could possibly act in such a disgraceful way?* It is the situation of severe persecution, when the acknowledgment of being a Christian can result in violent death. It is the situation of being brought before a Roman magistrate and being told, "If you will deny Christ, I will let you go."

Polycarp, who had exhorted the Philippian Christians to "carry out the word of righteousness and to practice endurance to the limit," was called to experience martyrdom as an old man. The account of his death is preserved in the form of a letter from the church of Smyrna to the church of Philomelium and is undoubtedly genuine. It has come to be known as the *Martyrdom of Polycarp*.

Polycarp appears to have been in his nineties when persecution broke out in Smyrna. When it became evident that a Roman festival would become an occasion for the severe harassment of Christians, a majority in the church persuaded their aged pastor to retire to a farm outside the city. There, in the company of a few friends, he spent his time in prayer.

Christians in Smyrna were arrested and brought before the Roman Pro-Consul, who sought to persuade them to take the oath of allegiance to the emperor, acknowledging Caesar as Lord, and to offer pagan sacrifice. A man named Quintus was remembered because "he played the coward" and complied, but most of the Christians from Smyrna remained true to Christ. They were scourged, burned alive, tortured on the rack, and torn by wild beasts. After a few days of this public spectacle, the crowd in the arena became restless and called for a search to be made for Polycarp.

Polycarp was moved to still another farm, but he could not remain hidden. A young slave revealed under torture where he could be found, and the police captain, with a detachment of cavalry, was dispatched to bring him to the arena. When Polycarp entered the arena there was a deafening roar from the spectators, but it could not drown out the heavenly voice which the aged pastor heard: "Be strong Polycarp, and play the man."

The Pro-Consul apparently had never seen Polycarp previously. When this venerable old man stood before him, he was deeply moved. He urged the old pastor to respect his age, and pressed him to take the oath, swearing by the genius of Caesar: "Take the oath and I will let you go. Revile Christ." Polycarp replied without hesitation: "For eighty-six years I have been his servant, and he has never wronged me. How can I blaspheme my King who saved me?" (*Martyrdom of Polycarp*, 9:3). When every effort at dissuasion had failed, the Pro-Consul sent his herald into the arena to announce three times, "Polycarp has confessed that he is a Christian." It was decreed that Polycarp should be burned alive. He was bound and consigned to the flames.

Polycarp is remembered for having listened to the voice of God. He fashioned his entire life out of the habit of obedience. By the time the ultimate crisis came, his moral faculty had been disciplined by constant practice to discriminate between ultimate good and evil. To have accepted release under the conditions offered to him would have been morally evil because it would have confirmed a pagan world in its blatant unbelief. It would have been like crucifying the Son of God again, because it would mean consenting with those who nailed him to the cross. It would have signified a willingness to hold Christ up to public contempt. Polycarp refused such an unacceptable release.

In historical documents of this period it was customary to fix a significant date by reference to the high priest of the Roman state religion, the provincial pro-consul, and the reigning emperor. The *Martyrdom of Polycarp* follows this pattern, with a striking difference:

Now the blessed Polycarp was martyred on the second day of the first half of the month of Xanthicus, the seventh day before the kalends of March, a great sabbath, at the eighth hour. And he was arrested by Herod, when Philip of Tralles was high priest, when Statius Quadratus was Pro-Consul, *but Jesus Christ was reigning for ever*, to whom be glory, honor, majesty and an eternal throne, from generation to generation. Amen (*Martyrdom of Polycarp*, 21).

From the perspective of the confessing church in Smyrna, Polycarp's obedience and fidelity in openly confessing Jesus as Lord had the effect of deposing the reigning emperor and enthroning Jesus Christ as sovereign in his place.

The dramatically different response of the coward Quintus, who accepted release from a violent death by reviling Christ and confessing Caesar as Lord (*Martyrdom of Polycarp*, 4), illustrates that in the situation of severe persecution a Christian could act in a disgraceful way. Quintus loved his life more than his Lord and denied Christ.

The preacher undoubtedly knew the tradition preserved for us in Mark 8:34-38. There Jesus spoke of circumstances in which a disciple might be tempted to preserve his life at any cost. It is possible to gain the approval of the whole world by holding Jesus Christ up to contempt. But the price of being ashamed of Jesus in this world is the forfeiture of eternal life, and the experience of rejection when the Son of Man comes in his Father's glory as the final Judge. No matter how great is the provocation, no matter how serious is the threat to human life, *there is no situation which would ever justify exposing Jesus Christ to public shame.*

(4) *Why is it impossible to restore to repentance the person who publicly denies his relationship with Jesus Christ?* It is impossible because the only ground upon which repentance can be offered to anyone is the action of God in Christ. If a Christian willfully repudiates that action, there is no other basis upon which repentance can be offered. The pastor's friends had learned that elementary truth when they were taught the foundational elements "consisting of repentance from works that lead to death and of faith in God" (6:1). That is why he urges, in 6:1: "Let us leave standing the elementary Christian teaching." Let the foundation remain standing because in the foundational truths there is a safeguard against the decision to save your life at the cost of being ashamed of your relationship with Jesus.

The sin that the preacher warns his friends to avoid is commonly called "apostasy." It is a sin that only a Christian can commit. *Apostasy consists in a deliberate, planned, intelligent decision to renounce publicly association with Jesus Christ.* It signifies a choice not to believe God, not to listen to God, not to obey God. It is the decision to be disobedient and to deny all that Christ has done for you. *The peril of spiritual immaturity is that a Christian can deliberately choose to reject the gifts of God received through Christ after he has experienced them.*

The verses which immediately follow, verses 7-8, are part of the larger context of 6:4-6. These verses place this stern warning in the perspective of the relationship with God defined by the covenant. They speak of "blessing" and "curse," terminology which brings us before God who establishes a covenant with his people. In the structure of an ancient covenant, such as the covenant enacted at Sinai, the promise of blessing is the divine response to obedience, but the sanction of a curse is the consequence for disobedience. The reference to blessing and curse in verses 7-8 places the discussion of apostasy in 6:4-6 in the framework of *covenant blessing* and *covenant curse.*

Christians have been related to God through Jesus Christ, the mediator of the new covenant (cf. 9:15). They have already experienced the blessings of the new covenant enumerated in 6:4-5. Describing their condition, the preacher makes use of an agricultural metaphor. He says in verse 7, We are like a fertile field that has been richly watered with the blessing of frequent rain. Now we must respond appropriately with obedience; that is, to be like a fertile field "which yields a useful crop to those for whom it is cultivated." That appropriate response will invite even more blessing (v. 7).

Conversely, a Christian who has experienced the rich array of blessings enumerated in 6:4-5, but who "has fallen away," is like a fertile field which has soaked up the blessing of frequent rain which falls upon it, yet produces only thorns and thistle, the tokens of a land which stands under a curse (Gen. 3:17-18). In reference to such a field the preacher comments sharply, "it is useless, and a curse hangs over it; in the end it will be burned over" (v. 8). The repudiation of Christ and the exposure of him to public shame through an act of apostasy would signify radical unbelief and profound disobedience which make inevitable the imposing of the curse sanctions of the covenant. Those who "have fallen away" after experiencing so many blessings can have only one expectation: their end will be rejection.

The pastor does not leave the matter there. Because he loved the people of God he had to speak to them the truth of God. Because he loved them deeply, he had to speak the truth even when it appeared to be severe. But he does not allow his friends to be confronted only by the severity of the truth. In the final paragraph of the first unit (6:9-12) he brings them before the mercy of the truth of God, and once again the tone is optimistic: "But even though we speak like this, dear friends, in your case we remain sure of the better things which accompany your salvation" (v. 9). The comforting words, "we remain sure," find their basis in the pastor's confidence that a genuine work of God has taken place among his friends.

It was necessary to warn them sternly of their peril because they had become "hard of hearing" and were exhibiting spiritual immaturity (5:11-14). *Nevertheless they displayed clear evidence of God's blessing.* With the warm expression of affection, "dear friends," which occurs only here in the sermon, the severity of 6:4-8 is softened. The reference to "the better things which accompany your salvation" has in view the better of the two options contemplated in verses 7-8. They are the well-watered and cultivated field which is capable of producing a useful harvest for God. *The preacher is persuaded that the commitment displayed by the community is genuine.*

The ground for the preacher's persuasion was the conduct of the community in the past, and in the present. He writes: "For God is not so unjust as to overlook your work and the love which you demonstrated with regard to him when you served, and continue to serve fellow Christians" (v. 10). The reference to past service appears to be to a period early in the experience of the community when they had displayed boldness before their persecutors, practical concern for those abused or imprisoned, and cheerful acceptance of the seizure of their property (10:32-34). They had demonstrated a loyalty to Christ that was an expression of firm faith and compelling hope, as well as of sincere Christian love. In 6:9-12 those same virtues of Christian character are placed before the congregation: *love* expressed in the service of fellow Christians (v. 10), the realization of *hope* (v. 11), and the quality of *faith* and steadfast endurance which inherits the promises of God (v. 12).

The final admonition of the first unit is addressed to each person in the house-church:

> But we want each one of you to demonstrate the same earnest concern with regard to the realization of your hope until the end, so that you will not become sluggish, but imitators of those who with faith and steadfast endurance inherit the promises (vv. 11-12).

In specifying "each one of you" the preacher stresses that *they are all to display the same concern* for the realization of their hope they had shown on that earlier occasion when they "endured a hard contest with sufferings" (10:32). The extended appeal in 5:11—6:12 is not to cast aside their hope, but to hold it confidently until it is realized. The motivating concern that undergirds the appeal is to prevent the congregation from becoming *sluggish* (v. 12). With this striking descriptive term the writer returns full circle to the point from where he began the unit: "You have become *sluggish* in your ears" (5:11).

The alternative to sluggishness, with its inherent peril, is to become "imitators of those who with faith and steadfast endurance inherit the promises" (v. 12*b*). The pastor has in mind especially the patriarch Abraham, whose example of faith and steadfast endurance is set forth in 6:13-15. With the final clause of verse 12 he concludes on a positive note the long unit concerning spiritual immaturity and constructs a bridge to the second unit of the section (6:13-20), where he establishes *a basis for Christian confidence and steadfastness*.

It is not necessary for the people of faith to collapse under the pressures to which they are exposed. A firm basis for confident steadfastness has been provided in the utter reliability of God's word of promise. It is presupposed in 6:13-20 that the new people of God enjoy continuity with Abraham as heirs to the divine word of promise. The preacher's optimism that his friends can recover their prior stance of confidence based on their past experience and future expectations is shown to rest upon the word of God's promise and oath.

The pastor reminds his friends of an awesome moment of assurance in the past when God said to Abraham, "Yes, I will certainly bless you and give you numerous descendants" (Gen. 22:17). This solemn promise, which was strengthened by an oath (Heb. 6:13), reaffirmed God's earlier promise that Abraham's descendants would be as innumerable as the stars of the heavens (Gen. 15:5). Abraham received this fresh affirmation of the divine promise after the incomprehensible command of God to sacrifice his son Isaac (Gen. 22:1-2) had placed in jeopardy God's earlier promise and called into question God's character and veracity.

On a day destined for dismay God had called Abraham by name and said to him: "Take your son, your only son Isaac, whom you love, and go to the region of Moriah. Sacrifice him there as a burnt offering on one of the mountains I will tell you about" (Gen. 22:2). Abraham had made listening to the voice of God the dominant disposition of his life. If there was ever a time when he would have wanted to close his ears and become "hard of hearing," it was at that moment. Nevertheless, listening to the voice of God had become the fixed habit of his life, and Abraham obeyed. His obedience required personal courage, firm trust in the character of God, and steadfastness of purpose. His faith must have been stretched beyond measure. When he left Ur of the Chaldees he turned his back upon his entire past. But when he was commanded to sacrifice Isaac it must have seemed that he was turning his back upon his entire future. The fulfillment of the divine promise concerning numerous descendants depended upon Isaac's life. In obedience, Abraham prepared to comply with a command he could not possibly understand.

In response to Abraham's remarkable faith and obedience on this painful occasion, the promise was reaffirmed and confirmed with an oath:

I swear by myself, declares the Lord, that because you have done this and have not withheld your son, your only son, I will surely bless you and make your descendants as numerous as the stars in the sky and as the sand on the seashore (Gen. 22:16-17).

God gave to his word the form of an oath in order to demonstrate the unchangeable character of his determination to do what he has promised. The preacher alludes to Genesis 22:16-17 when he comments, "And thus after steadfast endurance, Abraham received the promise" (v. 15). In the context of Abraham's experience in Genesis 22, "steadfast endurance" implies undeviating trust in a situation of severe testing.

In appealing to Abraham as an example of trust and steadfast endurance in 6:13-15, the preacher brings before his friends the venerable patriarch who lived his life in response to the promise of God. Abraham's experience, even when he could not understand God, demonstrated that God can be trusted. His word of promise is fully reliable.

The new element that is introduced with this illustration *is the reference to God's oath*. The divine oath is an expression of the intensity of God's speaking. It signifies the extent to which God commits himself to his spoken word. God's oath solemnly guarantees that he will fulfill his promises and that his word is truth. Accommodating himself to the human need for confirmation, the word of promise confirmed by an oath reveals the unchangeable character of God's will. An oath provides strong encouragement for his people to trust him with unwavering confidence. *God cannot lie in what he has said he will do* (vv. 16-18a).

In verse 17-18 the preacher underscores the relevance of his illustration for the members of the house-church:

Because God wanted to make especially plain to the heirs of the promise the irrevocable character of his resolve, he confirmed it by means of an oath, so that by two irrevocable facts, in which it is impossible for God to lie, we who have fled for refuge might have strong incentive to hold fast to the hope that is set in front of us.

The two "irrevocable facts" are God's promise and his solemn oath. God's resolve, which also is "irrevocable" in character, is to bring the heirs of the promise into the experience of their inheritance. The description of believers as those who have fled for refuge to God underscores the fact that God alone is the ground of Christian security. Sustained by God's promise and his confirming oath, Christians have strong incentive to hold fast to the hope which God has set before them as an objective gift extended to his people through Christ.

The reference to Christian hope in verse 18 sounds once again a note first introduced in 6:11. In concluding his exposition of the peril of spiritual immaturity, the preacher had urged his friends to hold firmly to the hope that they had received through the preaching of the gospel. Christian hope will be realized because it is grounded in objective reality. That theme is now developed, first with a nautical metaphor and then with a bold personification of hope:

We have this hope as an anchor for life, safe and secure. It enters the inner sanctuary behind the curtain, where Jesus has entered on our behalf as forerunner, having become a high priest forever, just like Melchizedek (vv. 19-20).

The comparison of hope to an anchor was common in the Mediterranean world. As a ship is held fast when at anchor, even in a squall, the lives of Christians are made safe and secure by the hope that binds them to Christ. The objective content of Christian hope lends stability to Christian life in an unstable world.

The bold depiction of Christian hope entering behind the curtain of the heavenly sanctuary, where Christ has entered as high priest in the presence of God, provides assurance that through our hope we may draw near to God and find in him the safe refuge we are seeking (cf. 4:15-16). The preacher will take up this thought again when he refers to "a new hope by which we draw near to God" (7:19). The present time of stress is simultaneously the time of sure and steadfast hope because through his sacrificial death Jesus has entered the presence of God on our behalf. The salvation he secured is guaranteed for the people of God by the utterly reliable promise of God. God's unchanging promise is the basis for Christian steadfastness.

It is now possible to review the entire section. The severity of the warning in 5:11—6:12 is thoroughly understandable. The preacher addressed a situation in which his friends had become sluggish and unreceptive to the claims of the gospel. They seemed to be unwilling to accept the deeper implications of God's claim upon their lives. They had regressed from a level of spiritual maturity attained over a period of years. These developments, which appear to be of relatively recent origin, were symptoms of a serious erosion of faith and hope. They called into question the integrity of the group and threatened to subvert and destroy their Christian witness. If the tendency to drift from their commitment to the gospel was not checked, they might flagrantly and contemptuously reject the worth of the sacrifice of Christ.

The congregation needed to be reminded that there was only one sufficient sacrifice for sins, and one basis upon which repentance could be extended to men and women. By writing from a distance, and dependent upon the power of the written word alone, the preacher had to address them in terms that would expose the peril of spiritual immaturity and recall them to their earlier stance of confidence in their experience and expectations. Pastoral concern for his friends is evident in every line of this extended section. The writer makes use of biting irony, confident assurance, sharp warning, and warm encouragement to coax the community into recognizing that they cannot turn back the clock and deny the reality of the salvation they have experienced.

In 6:13-20 the preacher presents Abraham as an example of trust and steadfast endurance. But he strengthens this example. He describes God's promise and oath to Abraham as a type of the way in which God relates himself to the Christian community. The promise to bless Abraham anticipates the salvation which God has given to the new people in Jesus. Abraham's experience with God demonstrated that God is faithful, that his words are reliable, and that he stands behind his promises. The promised salvation secured through the high priestly ministry of Jesus is certain because it is guaranteed by God's spoken word. This salvation is the objective content of the Christian hope which lends stability to God's people in a volatile situation.

In the two units of this section the preacher places before his friends the options of peril or promise. At the same time he prepares them for the exposition of Christ as priest and sacrifice. These themes will be developed under the aspect of an event of promise in which Christians have been invited to share by the grace of God.

VII

God's Son, Our Priest
(Hebrews 7:1-28)

The confession that "God's Son is our Priest" is possible only on the basis of Hebrews. Nowhere else in the New Testament is Jesus designated a priest or high priest. There are, to be sure, aspects of Jesus' ministry in the Gospels which might encourage us to think in the categories of priesthood. John 17, for example, has been described as "the high-priestly prayer of Jesus." There Jesus comes into the presence of the Father and prays for himself, for his own disciples, and for those who will come to the experience of faith through their witness. *Intercessory prayer is priestly action*, and John 17 certainly records a significant moment in Jesus' ministry of prayer which has priestly overtones. But the evangelist John never refers to Jesus as a priest. Only in Hebrews is Jesus designated a priest or high priest. The actual designation is the basis of the confession that God's Son is our Priest.

It is a striking fact that in Hebrews Jesus is described as a high priest before any clarification has been offered for the appropriateness of this designation. The expression "high priest" occurs for the first time in 2:17: "It was essential for him to be made like these brothers of his in every respect, in order that he might become a merciful and faithful *high priest* in the service of God." After this initial reference the designation recurs, significantly, at the opening and close of the sections which follow, 3:1—4:14 and 4:15—5:10.

3:1-2 For this reason...observe that the apostle and *high priest* of whom our confession speaks, Jesus, was faithful to the one who appointed him in his house.

101

4:14   Therefore, since we have a great *high priest* who has gone into heaven, Jesus the Son of God, let us continue to hold fast to our confession.

4:15   For we do not have a *high priest* who is unable to feel our weaknesses with us, but one who has been tested in every respect, in quite the same way as we are.

5:10   Being designated by God a *high priest*, just like Melchizedek.

Not until 5:1-10 is any explanation provided for this distinctive way of referring to Jesus. There it is shown that certain facets of experience which are true of every *high priest* are true of Jesus as well, and a biblical basis for designating Jesus a priest is provided with Psalm 110:4. *The fact that Jesus is designated a high priest prior to 5:1-10 may indicate that this congregation had begun to reflect on Jesus in priestly terms prior to receiving this sermon.*

The value of Hebrews is that certain aspects of Jesus' high priestly ministry are set forth and developed for the first time in a manner which enables us to understand the significance of describing Jesus as priest, or high priest. In fact the heart of the sermon, which extends from 7:1—10:18, is devoted to clarifying the high priestly office of Jesus.

In 7:1-28 the preacher explains for the first time why he describes Jesus as a high priest *like Melchizedek. The fullness of the explanation indicates that this is new teaching*. There is not a hint of this understanding anywhere else in the New Testament. It is evident that the Spirit of God has led the writer to grasp an aspect of the truth that had not been disclosed previously. If we did not possess Hebrews this dimension of Jesus' character would have been closed to us. It is an important dimension. When the preacher says that Jesus is a high priest *like Melchizedek* he is making two declarations: (1) Jesus' appointment to the high priestly office was the action of God; (2) Jesus is a unique high priest because God raised him from the dead. If he had not been raised from the dead, he would not have been qualified to be our high priest. *Both of these insights are affirmed when Jesus is described as a high priest like Melchizedek.*

Melchizedek is an historical figure who is remembered in Scripture because of a single incident in the life of the patriarch Abraham. The account of the incident is found in Genesis 14. In the course of quelling a rebellion, Kedorlaomer, the king of Elam, and his allies raided Sodom and plundered the city. Among the captives who were carried off was Abraham's nephew, Lot. With a small army Abraham pursued the marauding kings, overpowered them, rescued Lot, and captured the spoils of war. On his return from this engagement Abraham met the king of Sodom and Melchizedek, the king of the city-state of Salem (Gen. 14:17-20).

Melchizedek is distinguished from his companion, the king of Sodom, by the fact that he was both a king and a priest; he was king of Salem and "priest of God Most High" (Gen. 14:18). *He may be described as a royal priest*. The fact that in the person of Melchizedek the offices of king and priest were combined is unusual precisely because after the giving of the law at Sinai, and throughout Israel's later history, the offices of king and priest were established as separate spheres of leadership. The law mandated that kings were not to engage in priestly service, and priests were not to function as kings. Melchizedek, however, is both king and priest.

Melchizedek is distinguished also by the fact that *he is the first priest mentioned in the Bible*. He functioned as a priest long before the appointment of Aaron as Israel's first high priest. The designation of Melchizedek as a "priest of God Most High" indicates that he had been appointed to the priestly office by God. Melchizedek brought out bread and wine with which he refreshed Abraham and his men, and he pronounced a blessing upon Abraham and upon God Most High who was responsible for Abraham's success (Gen. 14:19-20). *The one priestly function that is associated with Melchizedek in Genesis 14 is the action of blessing Abraham*. In recognition of the priestly dignity of Melchizedek, Abraham gave him a tenth of the spoils of war he had captured (Gen. 14:20c).

This brief episode contains the only reference to Melchizedek in the stories of the patriarchs preserved in the book of Genesis. He met Abraham, refreshed him, and pronounced a blessing upon him, and then recedes into the shadows of history, while Abraham continues to occupy the center of the stage in Genesis.

Abraham lived during the period near the year 2000 BC. For a thousand years no one appears to have remembered that shadowy figure, the priest-king of Salem, Melchizedek. There is no mention of him in the subsequent history of Israel, until the tenth century BC, when David, under the inspiration of the Holy Spirit, composed Psalm 110. In Psalm 110:4 we read: "The Lord has sworn; he will not change his mind, 'You are a priest forever, just like Melchizedek.' " This remarkable statement occurs at a time when the Levitical priesthood had been divinely established for about 350 years. They were a highly visible presence in the life of Israel. *Now God declares that he is going to do something new.* He is going to bring into history an individual who will be a priest *like Melchizedek. Like Melchizedek,* he will owe his appointment to the action of God. *Like Melchizedek* he will be both king and priest. Moreover, God swears that he will be *a priest forever.* The fulfillment of this sworn promise is guaranteed by the divine oath: "The Lord has sworn; he will not change his mind" (Psalm 110:4). The oath serves to emphasize the unchangeable character of God's purpose.

The unexpected reference to Melchizedek prompts a whole series of questions. Why does God speak of a different priesthood, at a time when the Levitical priesthood continued to exercise a felt presence in the life of Israel? Why does God reach back to the period of Abraham when he wants to suggest a model for this new priesthood? Why does he say, "You are a priest...just like Melchizedek"? What was true of Melchizedek that explains why the Spirit of God caused this mysterious person who met Abraham and blessed him to be remembered one thousand years after that brief encounter?

The answer to these questions must take into account an important consideration. There was a fundamental difference between Melchizedek and the Levitical priests. The appointment of the Levitical high priest was regulated by the Mosaic Law. According to the Law, the high priest had to be able to trace a line of physical descent back to Aaron on his father's side. His mother had to be a pure Israelite woman. The key questions to be asked were, "Who is your father?" "Who is your mother?" "Do you trace your line of physical descent back to Aaron on your father's side?" But Melchizedek was a priest through the direct appointment of God. He had no qualification for priesthood other than the divine appointment. This is a crucial consideration in the interpretation of Hebrews 7:1-25: *Melchizedek is a priest not through legal qualification but by the appointment of God.*

There is a second fundamental difference between Melchizedek and the Levitical priests. There was a succession of Levitical priests. After Aaron's death, his office was filled by Eleazar, his son. After Eleazar's death, the office was occupied by his son, Phinehas. *There was an established line of succession to the high priesthood.* For every high priest after Aaron, there was a predecessor in the high priestly office and there was a successor. *But this is not true of Melchizedek.* Scripture does not refer to any predecessor, and it is silent concerning any successor. He appears in the record as a priest of God in a specified moment of history, and he has no successor. For that reason whenever one thinks of Melchizedek in terms of Scripture, it is necessary to think of him as possessing *a permanent priesthood. His priesthood was not passed on to another.*

Two considerations, then, explain why God speaks of a new kind of priesthood in Psalm 110:4 when he promises the coming of one who is a priest like Melchizedek. (1) *He will be a priest who owes his appointment to God rather than to the law of physical descent.* (2) *He will enjoy a permanent priesthood,* acknowledged in the formula, "You are a priest forever." Both of these considerations were important to the preacher who wrote Hebrews. They become crucial categories when he speaks of the priesthood of Jesus for *they demonstrate that Jesus is a priest like Melchizedek.*

Structurally, Hebrews 7:1-28 consists of three units. In 7:1-10 the preacher introduces the person of Melchizedek, focusing attention on the details of Genesis 14:17-20. In 7:11-25 Psalm 110:4 is brought prominently into the argument to advance the discussion toward the consideration of the priest who is like Melchizedek, the person of Jesus. In a concluding paragraph, 7:26-28, the writer moves beyond the biblical passages in order to construct a bridge to the exposition of Jesus as our priest and sacrifice in 8:1—10:18.

The function of the first unit (7:1-10), then, is to clarify the significance of the mysterious figure in Abraham's past, Melchizedek. The unit displays a concentric symmetry which can be exhibited in a chart:

7:1-3

A The meeting with Abraham (v. 1*a*).
B The blessing bestowed (v. 1*b*).
C The tithe received (v. 2).

7:4-10

C' The tithe received (v. 4).
B' The blessing bestowed (v. 6).
A' The meeting with Abraham (v. 10).

By introducing three points of contact between Abraham and Melchizedek, and then reviewing them in inverse order, the pastor assists his friends to become involved in discovering the significance of this episode from the past.

The preacher summarizes what can be known about Melchizedek from Genesis 14 in verses 1-2, and he comments briefly on the meaning of his name ("King of righteousness") and of his royal title ("King of peace"). He then draws important implications from the biblical account in verse 3: "His father, mother, and line of descent are unknown, and there is no record of his birth or of his death, but having been made to resemble the Son of God, he remains a priest continuously." This statement is crucial, for it indicates the insights that the preacher received from the Spirit of God as he reflected upon Melchizedek. Each of the clauses deserves careful consideration.

In the first part of the statement ("his father, mother, and line of descent are unknown"), the preacher is commenting that there is no genealogical record which serves as the basis of his priesthood. He is "without father" and "without mother" because no mention is made of his father, mother, or family line in Genesis. *The silence of Scripture* concerning Melchizedek's parents and family line is stressed in verse 3 because this fact throws into bold relief the uniqueness of his priesthood. Melchizedek's priesthood was based solely upon the call of God, not on the hereditary process by which the Levitical priesthood was sustained. Without a recorded priestly genealogy, Melchizedek could not have qualified for Levitical priesthood. Nevertheless, this man was "priest of God Most High," and Abraham recognized his priestly office.

On the basis of the silence of Genesis concerning Melchizedek's birth or death ("there is no record of his birth or of his death") the preacher makes a second statement: the priesthood of Melchizedek had no beginning and no end. *Consequently, there was no Scriptural limitation to his life and work.* He did not require priestly ancestry nor priestly succession to authorize his unique and unending priesthood. Melchizedek's sudden appearance and equally sudden disappearance from recorded human history awakens within a sensitive reader the notion of eternity. This notion was merely prefigured in a suggestive way in Melchizedek, but it is realized in Christ. For this reason, Melchizedek foreshadows the priesthood of Christ at that point where it is most fundamentally different from the Levitical priesthood.

The third clause ("but having been made [by God] to resemble the Son of God") informs the congregation that the account of Melchizedek in Genesis 14 has been read from the perspective of the future reality it prefigured. The statement that Melchizedek has been made to resemble the Son of God means that the description of this ancient priest in verse 3 has been influenced by the preacher's understanding of God's eternal Son. He found reflected in the person of Melchizedek important features which would belong to the eternal priest, according to Psalm 110:4. *Melchizedek is thus an illustration of the higher priesthood promised in the Old Testament. He possesses prophetic significance;* in Melchizedek we have a prophecy that God will bring forward a different kind of priesthood.

The final clause goes beyond the statement of Genesis in endowing Melchizedek with a perpetual priesthood ("he remains a priest continuously"). The formulation shows that Genesis 14 has been read in the light of Psalm 110:4 ("You are a priest *forever*, like Melchizedek"). In Genesis 14 Melchizedek does not take up his priestly service from a predecessor and he remains a priest without a successor. The silence of the biblical record invests Melchizedek with a continuous priesthood which foreshadows the eternal and final character of the priesthood of Christ. *The continuing nature of Melchizedek's priesthood is it distinguishing feature.* It is this element which particularly interests the preacher as he prepares to present Jesus as the high priest "like Melchizedek."

The historical account in Genesis 14 implies the kind of priesthood that God intended to displace the Levitical priesthood. It suggested the ministry of an eternal priest who exercises his priesthood continuously. It anticipates the appearance of a high priest who does not have any successor because he does not require one. His priesthood is permanent in character. *The account looks forward to the coming of Christ.*

The point made in the continuation of the unit (7:4-10) is that Melchizedek is a priest who is superior to the Levitical priests. The basis of the argument is that Abraham paid a tithe to Melchizedek and was blessed by Melchizedek. These details from Genesis 14 demonstrate how great Melchizedek was (v. 4). *He was more exalted than the great patriarch Abraham.* As the patriarch of the Hebrew race, Abraham embodied and represented the entire group of his descendants. When he designates Abraham as "the patriarch" (v. 4), the preacher is stressing that Abraham is not simply an individual; *in this context he is a representative figure.* The term in verse 4 prepares for the conclusion in verse 9-10 that Levi actually paid a tithe to Melchizedek through his father Abraham. In that representative sense, even the Levitical order acknowledged Melchizedek's dignity. *The entire argument in verses 4-10 is intended to show how great Melchizedek was.*

The reason for this development becomes clear in the second unit (7:11-25). In this unit there is no further reference to Genesis 14; all of the interest is concentrated on Psalm 110:4. This inevitably means the center of attention will no longer be the person of Melchizedek but the promised priest who is like Melchizedek. What will be demonstrated in this unit is the insufficiency of the old Levitical priesthood and the sufficiency of the new priesthood.

In 7:11-25 the preacher is concerned to emphasize ways in which *Jesus is like Melchizedek*. Simultaneously, he underscores the ways in which *Jesus is not like the Levitical priests*. The Levitical priesthood was inadequate to bring the people of God to the goal God intended for them. That is why God promised a different priesthood in Psalm 110:4, the priesthood like that of Melchizedek. It is clear that the preacher read the prophetic oracle in Psalm 110:4 as a solemn decree of appointment spoken by God to the Son! It referred to the coming of Christ to perform a priestly ministry.

In this second unit the preacher is able to build upon what he has established about Melchizedek in 7:1-10. The course of the development unfolds in four steps.

Step One is taken in verses 11-12: *the prophecy of a new priesthood demonstrated that the old priesthood was insufficient.* It was insufficient because it was unable to bring the people to God's intended goal. Long after the Levitical priesthood was an established presence in the life of Israel, God spoke [in Psalm 110:4] of the installing of another priest. What is striking is that he is characterized as a priest *like Melchizedek*, not *like Aaron* (v. 11). That fact, in itself, indicated that God was announcing a change in the Law (v. 12).

Step Two follows in verses 13-14: *Psalm 110:4 was actually a prophecy of the coming of Jesus as our high priest.* We can now understand why God said, "You are a priest like Melchizedek." That formulation declares that the one about whom God was speaking did not satisfy the legal qualification of belonging to the tribe of Levi (v. 13). That is certainly true of Jesus. He was descended from Judah, and no provision was made in the Mosaic law for anyone from that tribe to serve the altar (v. 14). In fact, Moses never foresaw that this tribe would be appointed to priestly service.

It is clear that the new priest announced in Psalm 110:4 is different from the priests of Aaron's line. He enjoys his priestly office only because of the appointment of God announced in the oracle of Psalm 110:4. Step Two demonstrates that the new priest is different from Aaron and that he lacks the legal qualification of belonging to the tribe of Levi. Consequently, his priesthood must depend upon a profoundly new arrangement. The designation "our Lord" in verse 14 shows that the preacher is thinking of Jesus as he frames his argument. *Jesus is the new priest announced prophetically in Psalm 110:4.*

Step Three is found in verses 15-17: *the new priest is superior in quality to the priests of the Levitical order.* He possesses his priesthood not on the basis of a legal regulation concerning physical descent from Aaron but on the basis of the power of an indestructible life. The reference in verse 16 is to the resurrection of Jesus from the dead.

The preacher certainly knows that Jesus suffered death; he was exposed to destruction. There is repeated reference to the Cross of Christ in Hebrews. Consequently, when he describes Jesus as possessing an "indestructible life" he does not mean that Jesus never died. He means that he died a death that was unable to hold him. It was a death that was followed by the resurrection. To proclaim that Jesus is high priest on the basis of the power of an indestructible life is to say that he is high priest on the basis of his resurrection. This is the meaning of the words of God the Father to the Son in Psalm 110:4: "You are a priest forever, just like Melchizedek" (v. 17).

This is a striking, new perspective from which to consider Easter. At Easter Jesus was not only shown to be the Son of God with power through the resurrection from the dead, as declared in an old creedal formula cited in Romans 1:4. At Easter he was appointed by God to be our great high priest, who is alive, and who always lives to act in priestly service on behalf of his people. Because Jesus is alive, he has been appointed to an eternal priesthood. *He is an effective priest because he possesses a unique quality of life.*

The oracle of Psalm 110:4 had reference to a priest whose quality would be like Melchizedek as he is described in Genesis 14:18-20 and Psalm 110:4. The promise was fulfilled in Christ who is *actually* what Melchizedek was *symbolically;* namely an eternal priest who exercises his priestly ministry on our behalf.

Step Four is taken in verses 18-19: *the Levitical priesthood and the old Law have been set aside by the new and "better hope" based on the superior quality of the new priest.* The old priesthood and the old Law were set aside because they had been ineffective in achieving God's purpose. Their ineffectiveness is a reflection on the weakness of the persons upon whom the priesthood and the Law depended for the accomplishment of the divine purpose. The people of God failed to be brought into a right relationship with God through the cleansing of the conscience or the heart.

The old institutions of priesthood and sacrifice were unable to achieve a final and complete arrangement for relationship with God. That is why they *have been replaced by an effective hope* (vv. 18-19). The hope is effective ("better") because it is guaranteed by God's oath and by God's action in raising Jesus from the dead. It points forward to a direct and lasting access to God. We may draw near to God with confidence.

The pastoral implications of this four-step argument are drawn more fully in verses 20-25. Psalm 110:4 remains firmly embedded in the preacher's mind. In verses 20-22 he takes up the introduction to the oracle, "The Lord has sworn and will not change his mind," in order to contrast the new priest like Melchizedek with the old priesthood. In verses 23-25 he explores the significance of the prophetic announcement, "You are a priest forever," in order to sharpen the contrast between the new priest like Melchizedek and the old priesthood. *Each of these smaller units of the sermon sets forth a benefit* that the new arrangement brings to Christians because they have, in the person of Jesus, a superior priest.

(1) *The new covenant has a guarantor who assures its effectiveness, both for the present and for the future* (vv. 20-22). This benefit follows from the fact that the new priest was established in his office by the oath of God ("the Lord has sworn and will not change his mind"). His priesthood reflects God's unchangeable purpose. This cannot be said with reference to the priests of the old Levitical order. Jesus is the guarantor of the new arrangement. His death, exaltation, and installation as heavenly priest in response to the divine decree provides the guarantee that the new and better covenant will not be set aside. God's new work of salvation, which had its inception in the preaching of Jesus (2:3), finds its completion in the heavenly, high-priestly ministry of Jesus.

(2) *Since Jesus exercises an eternal and final priesthood, he is able to mediate an eternal and final salvation* (vv. 23-25). *Under the old arrangement* associated with Aaron and the Levitical line *there were many priests.* They were prevented from remaining in office by the simple fact of death. As a result of death, the course of the Levitical priesthood was repeatedly disrupted. *Under the new arrangement* associated with Jesus *there is only one priest* who has been invested with an eternal and final priesthood. The declaration that "he continues forever" (v. 24) indicates that he enjoys *a permanent priesthood.* In contrast to the Levitical priests, whose ministry was constantly disrupted by death, there is no disruption and no limitation to the ministry of a priest who lives forever! He is qualified to exercise a ministry that is permanent and final.

What, precisely, is the character of Jesus' priestly ministry? The preacher anticipates this question and begins to answer it in verse 25 by underlining two related aspects of priestly ministry.

(1) *He is "able to save absolutely" those who approach God through him.* The preacher's statement implies that Jesus' priestly support is available at each critical moment in our lives. He has a sustained concern for the welfare of his people. The fullness and completeness of the salvation he secured for us is guaranteed by the eternal character of his priesthood.

(2) *He is able to approach the Father on behalf of his people.* The function of the priest in the life of Israel was to speak to God on behalf of the people. Prayer is a distinctly priestly action. The fact that our heavenly high priest lives continually signifies that his capacity for effectively acting on behalf of his people is unlimited. He is able to meet every need of the Christian because he is the permanent intercessor for his people. The indestructible life of the Son (v. 16) is the basis for his uninterrupted priestly intercession. As one who is profoundly involved with our lives, he proves to be effective, when, in fact, the Levitical priests were not because their priestly service was interrupted by death. *His responsibility* is unceasing intercession; *our responsibility* is to approach God through him.

In the final paragraph (7:26-28) the preacher moves beyond the warrant of Psalm 110:4 in order to speak of the sinless character and sacrificial death of the new high priest. His statement is informed by reflection on God's provision for a sin-offering on the solemn Day of Atonement. In this setting he emphasizes still a third aspect of Jesus' priestly ministry.

(3) *He offered the perfect sacrifice when he offered to God his life,
once for all, as an unblemished sacrifice* (v. 27). The offering of sacrifice is, of course, a distinctly priestly function. Our high priest
made the definitive sacrifice for sins because he was sinless in his
character (7:26; cf. 4:15). His own sinlessness explains why no
sin offering was required from him, as it was of the Levitical high
priests. His sinlessness guarantees the effectiveness of his atoning
death.

In order to introduce this third aspect of priestly ministry it
was necessary for the preacher to move beyond the warrant of
Genesis 14 and Psalm 110:4 because in Scripture Melchizedek
has no connection with sacrifice. The tantalizingly brief reference to Jesus' sacrificial ministry in verse 27 looks forward to the
fuller development of this theme in 9:11-14, where the preacher
will clarify the significance of Jesus' sacrificial death. Here already it is clearly implied that *his unique offering of himself put an
end to the whole Levitical system of sacrifices.* The fact that Christ
offered himself "once for all" signifies the completeness of his
sacrifice for sins.

The preacher's own moving response to the entire argument is
the spontaneous declaration in verse 26, "Now such a high priest
was precisely appropriate for us." The remarkable traits ascribed
to him demonstrate Jesus' qualification to be the true high priest:
he was qualified religiously ("one who is devout); *he was qualified
morally* ("one who is guileless"); *and he was qualified in terms of
cultic purity* ("one who is undefiled"). He is fully qualified to
come into the presence of God in priestly action. His life among
sinners ceased with his ascension. He has left the sphere characterized by testing, hostility, and suffering, and "having been separated from sinners" he has been exalted to the presence of God
where he ministers as our heavenly high priest. Such a high
priest is "appropriate"because he is sensitive to the circumstances
that threaten to fragment the members of the house-church, and
he is able to minister to all of their needs and inadequacies.

A final summary statement brings the course of the argument
to a head with a series of contrasts (v. 28).

(1) The basis of the old priesthood was the law concerning
physical descent from Aaron; the basis of the new priesthood is
the word of God's sworn oath, as attested in Psalm 110:4.

(2) The old priesthood consisted of men liable to death; the
new priest is the eternal Son of God, whose exercise of priesthood is sustained by the power of an indestructible life.

(3) The old priests were "affected by weakness" in the form of imperfections and sin; the new priest "has been made perfect forever," which signifies that he is fully qualified to come before God in priestly action on our behalf. In contrast to men who are weak we are to contemplate the strong Son of God, who validates the priestly character of his mission through a series of events climaxed by the offering of himself to God as an unblemished sacrifice.

In summary, then, the old arrangement of salvation suffered from a shortness of spiritual breath and has been completely set aside. It has been replaced with the new and final priesthood of Jesus which is endowed with a quality of life that is unaffected by death. *The new priesthood is qualitatively different from the old because it is a fully effective priesthood.*

There is a distinctly practical orientation to the exposition of the old biblical texts which refer to Melchizedek. The preacher's friends appear to have doubted the ability of God to act decisively in the present on their behalf. In response to their doubts, he stresses both the reality of God's final action in Christ and Christ's present ability to help them face the realities of their situation. The affirmation that the Son of God is able to save absolutely those who approach God through him (v. 25) signifies that *he is able to save in the present and to the end*. His exercise of an uninterrupted priestly ministry of prayer assures us of final and complete salvation.

For a priest to be fully effective he must have continual access to the presence of God. The exalted status of God's Son, our heavenly high priest, assures us that the objectives of his eternal priesthood will be completely realized.

VIII

God's Son, Our Sacrifice
(Hebrews 8:1—9:28)

Watch The Lamb

In Hebrews 7:1-25 the preacher demonstrated the superior character of Jesus' priesthood by comparing him to Melchizedek. Like Melchizedek he owed his *appointment* to God. Like Melchizedek, he possesses a *permanent* priesthood. Like Melchizedek, he exercises a *unique* priesthood. He possesses his priesthood on the basis of the power of an indestructible life.

Jesus is our high priest on the basis of his resurrection. Although his life had been exposed to destruction when he was put to death on the cross, death could not hold him. God raised him from the dead and appointed him to be our great high priest. He is alive, and because he lives he is able to act effectively in priestly service on behalf of the people of God. *He is a fully effective priest because he possesses a unique quality of life.* The comparison with Melchizedek, then, is suggestive of the distinctive character of the priesthood exercised by God's Son.

There is a significant aspect of Jesus' priestly ministry, however, which is not illumined by the comparison with Melchizedek. That aspect concerns Jesus' presentation of his life to God as an unblemished sacrifice. In Scripture Melchizedek has no association with sacrifice. If this sacrificial aspect of Jesus ministry is to be emphasized a different comparison must be developed. It is to the development of that comparison that the preacher turns in 8:1—9:28. *He compares the priestly action of Jesus with the action of the Levitical high priest on the annual Day of Atonement.* On that solemn occasion the high priest entered the Most High Place of the tabernacle and stood in the awesome presence of God to make atonement for the sins of the people.

The account of the establishment of an annual Day of Atonement is to be found in Leviticus 16. It was to be a day of fasting

114

and self-denial, "because on this day atonement will be made for you, to cleanse you" (Lev. 16:30). On that day the congregation of Israel was to be cleansed from the defilement of sin. It was to be a day that would affect profoundly the lives of all of the people:

The priest who is anointed...is to put on the sacred linen garments and make atonement for the Most Holy Place, for the Tent of Meeting and the altar, and for the priests and all the people of the community (Lev. 16:32-33).

It was to be a day that was observed once every year: "This is to be a lasting ordinance for you: Atonement is to be made once a year for all the sins of the Israelites" (Lev. 16:34).

An allusion to the solemn Day of Atonement and to the significant action of the high priest on that day stands behind the preacher's development of the theme, God's Son, our Sacrifice. This is evident already in Hebrews 7:27, where a comparison is drawn between the Levitical high priests and God's Son. On the Day of Atonement the Levitical high priest had to offer a sacrifice first for his own sins, and then he presented an offering for the sins of the people. In fact, his sin offering was a young bull (Lev. 16:6, 11-14); the sin offering for the people was a goat (Lev. 16:15). *Accordingly, once each year the high priest had to acknowledge that he was implicated in the defilement of sin which characterized all the people of God*, as he offered sacrifice first for his own sins and then for the sins of the people.

But God's Son was not like the Levitical high priests. He did not have to offer a sin offering for his own sin (7:27a) because he was "devout, guileless, and undefiled" (7:26). *Precisely for that reason he was qualified to offer the definitive sacrifice on behalf of those whom he represented*. The preacher declares emphatically, "He sacrificed for their sins once for all when he offered himself" (7:27b). His unique offering of himself put an end to the whole Levitical system of sacrifices because he secured complete atonement.

With this background it is possible to provide a rapid overview of 8:1—9:10. In this section of the sermon *the preacher relates the conception of Jesus as a heavenly high priest to the themes of sanctuary and covenant*. His intention is to prepare his friends for the core of his message in 9:11-28.

As the section is introduced the preacher announces his most important point:

Now the crowning affirmation of what we are saying is this: We do have such a high priest, who has taken his seat at the right hand of the throne of the Majesty in heaven, the ministering priest of the sanctuary, of the true tabernacle, which the Lord pitched, not man (8:1-2).

This triumphant declaration introduces two significant comparisons which call attention to Christ in his office as ministering priest (8:1-5) and to Christ in his office as mediator of the new covenant (8:6-13). In the initial paragraph the pastor characterizes *the new ministry (8:1-2), which is set in opposition to the old Levitical ministry* (8:3-5). In the following paragraph he affirms that the new ministry introduces *a better covenant* (8:6), which *is set in opposition to the old covenant* (8:7-13).

The point established in 8:1-5 is that we have a heavenly high priest. The place of his ministry is not the earthly sanctuary of the tabernacle but the heavenly sanctuary, where he is enthroned at God's right hand. There is in verse 3 just a hint of the later presentation of Christ's sacrificial ministry in the concession that this heavenly priest "had necessarily something to offer." At this point in the sermon, however, there is no elaboration of this notion. Instead, the argument focuses sharply on the difference between the Levitical high priests and the final priest: they serve a sanctuary that is only a shadowy suggestion of the heavenly sanctuary; his ministry is in the sanctuary which God erected. *The reference to the earthly sanctuary and to the heavenly sanctuary shows that the new ministry of Christ is being compared favorably to the old Levitical ministry by focusing attention on the character of the sanctuary in which ministry is performed.*

In 8:6-13 the new ministry of Christ is associated with the new covenant which was enacted as a result of Christ's death on the cross:

In fact, the ministry which he has attained is as superior to theirs as the covenant of which he is a mediator is superior to the old one, seeing that this covenant has been drawn up on the basis of better promises (8:6).

The measure of the superiority of Jesus' ministry is expressed with a comparison based on the fact that Jesus entered the heavenly sanctuary as the mediator of the new covenant. Moses was the mediator of the old covenant. The new covenant, however, required a new mediator. By his life of perfect obedience and his death as a covenant sacrifice, Jesus inaugurated the new covenant promised by God in Jeremiah 31:31-34. His entrance into the heavenly sanctuary provides assurance that God has accepted his sacrifice and that the provisions of the superior covenant he mediates have been enacted. *The new priesthood and sacrifice provide the ground for the introduction of the new covenant.*

The prophetic oracle in which God promised to establish a new covenant with his people (Jer. 31:31-34) is cited in full in 8:8-12. This is the longest quotation from the Old Testament to be found in the New Testament. The preacher examines the promise that God will establish a new covenant from the perspective of Jeremiah's time, when the promise was first announced. The fact that God spoke to Jeremiah of a covenant that was *new* indicates that the *old* covenant was imperfect and provisional. *The old covenant was defective*; it developed faults on the human side. By qualifying the arrangement announced in Jeremiah 31:31-34 as "new," God treated the old Sinai covenant as obsolete and outdated (8:13). The announcement of the new covenant foreshadows that God's redemptive purpose will be realized through the mediator of the new covenant.

In the section that follows the preacher is concerned to develop the difference between the old covenant and the new covenant by comparing their respective provisions for worship. The provisions for worship under the old covenant are set forth in 9:1-10. The pastor remarks, "Now the first covenant had regulations for cultic worship and a sanctuary which was earthly"(9:1). The earthly sanctuary to which he refers, of course, was the tabernacle that was erected by Moses. In 9:2-5 he describes the arrangement of the tabernacle into two compartments: a front compartment called the Holy Place, and a rear compartment called the Most Holy Place. The purpose of this brief description of the two compartments of the tabernacle is to emphasize the provisions for worship afforded to the congregation of Israel. *The old sanctuary consisted of a system of barriers between the worshiper and God.*

In 9:6-10 the stress falls upon the limited access to God that was permitted under the old covenant. Only priests could enter the front compartment of the tabernacle, where they carried out their assigned ministries (v. 6). Entrance into the Most Holy Place, where God manifested his presence visibly through the *Shekinah* glory was even more restricted: "But only the high priest entered the rear compartment, and that only once a year, and never without blood, which he offers for himself and also for the sins the people had committed in ignorance" (v. 7). The reference is clearly to the Day of Atonement when the high priest represented the congregation in the awesome atonement ritual by entering the Most Holy Place. Every phrase underscores the limited access to God under the Levitical arrangement: "only the high priest"; "only once a year"; "never without blood."

The reference to "blood" in verse 7 is important. It marks the first use of this term in a cultic, sacrificial sense in the sermon. The instructions for the Day of Atonement describe sin as defilement and specify that sacrificial blood may act as a purging, or cleansing, agent (Lev. 16:15-16). Sacrificial blood is specified as the medium of approach to God. The requirement that entrance into the Most Holy Place must never be without "blood" noted in verse 7, prepares for the repeated reference to this significant term in 9:11-28, where the preacher speaks of the "blood" of Christ.

The point of referring to the priestly ministry in the two compartments of the tabernacle is made clear in verse 8: "The Holy Spirit was showing by this that the way into the real sanctuary had not yet been disclosed while the first compartment had cultic status." The Holy Spirit disclosed to the preacher that so long as this arrangement was valid, direct access to the presence of God was not yet available to the congregation. The people could approach God only through their representatives, the priests and high priest. The Levitical arrangement expressed in the tabernacle was actually a barrier to the presence of God. This was the first weakness in the provisions for worship under the old arrangement.

A second weakness is exposed in verses 9-10: the gifts and sacrifices which were offered in the earthly tabernacle were incapable of achieving a decisive cleansing of the conscience of the worshiper. The term "conscience" in Hebrews is used in a distinctive way. It describes the whole interior self; it reflects upon the relationship of the whole person to God. In the context of the worship of God, it is the smiting, burdened conscience that is in view, which effectively keeps a worshiper from God. In Hebrews, the function of the conscience is not to discriminate between right and wrong but to remember the sin that separates a worshiper from God. It exposed the truth that defilement extends to the heart as well as to the body, and that it erects a barrier to the living God. The inability of the gifts and sacrifices offered on the Day of Atonement and through the daily sacrifices to achieve a decisive cleansing of the conscience was, therefore, a serious weakness. Moreover, this deficiency affected all of the worshipers—priest and people alike.

The fact that the most solemn ceremonies of the old covenant, those of the annual Day of Atonement, had to be repeated every year demonstrated that the sacrifices which were offered could not achieve a permanent cleansing. The inadequacy of the old sacrifices justifies putting them on the same level as rather peripheral matters governing life in ancient Israel, regulations concerning food and drink and various ceremonial washings (v. 10).

The argument in 9:1-10 is designed to show that the provision for worship under the old covenant was only a temporary arrangement in the unfolding of God's redemptive purpose for his people. The tabernacle with its two compartments and the Levitical priesthood had validity only "until the time of correction" (v. 10) introduced by the incarnation and death of God's Son. Now that the new age has come with Christ, the regulations of the old covenant are no longer in force, and the earthly tabernacle with its provisions for worship has lost its significance and status.

In summary, in 9:1-10 the preacher demonstrates *two serious limitations* in the provisions for worship under the old covenant: (1) *the severe restriction of access to God indicated that the arrangement was provisional;* (2) *the inadequacy of the sacrifices offered to provide decisive cleansing indicated that the arrangement was imperfect.* The preacher thus sets the stage in 9:1-10 for the consideration of the ministry of Christ, the true and final high priest, in the heavenly sanctuary (9:11-28). Again, *the key issues which must be addressed are the provision of an adequate sacrifice and of unlimited access to God.* These issues are resolved in terms of the sacrificial ministry of Jesus.

An analysis of the argument in 9:11-28 shows that there are two major units of thought, the second of which is predicated upon the first. An overview is provided in outline form.

First Unit: The achievement of our high priest (9:11-14).
(1) He entered the heavenly sanctuary (v. 11).
(2) He obtained eternal salvation (v. 12).
(3) He has decisively cleansed the conscience (vv. 13-14).

Transition: Therefore he is the mediator of the new covenant (v. 15).

Second Unit: The basis for Christ's high priestly achievement (9:15-28).

(1) He is the mediator of the new covenant (v. 15).

Parenthetical explanation of why Christ had to die (vv. 16-22). The necessity of Christ's death (v. 16-17), is rooted in covenant practice (vv. 18-22).

(2) He exercises a heavenly high priestly ministry (vv. 23-28).

This outline recognizes that the initial paragraph (9:11-14) prepares for the conclusion that Christ is the mediator of the new covenant. The association of this mediatorial role with "a death having occurred for redemption from transgressions committed on the basis of the former covenant" (v. 15) poses the question: Why was it necessary for Christ to die? The long parenthesis which follows verse 15 (vv. 16-22) responds to that question in terms of covenantal practice. This explanation illumines verse 15 and leads directly into the final paragraph (vv. 23-28), where the significance of Christ's priestly ministry in heaven is clarified.

In defining the decisive achievement of our high priest *the preacher focuses upon the issues of sacrifice and sanctuary*. Christ did not approach God with the sacrificial blood of bulls and goats (as did the Levitical high priest on the Day of Atonement), but he did with his own blood (v. 12). *Consequently, he has been able to achieve decisive cleansing* (v. 14). He did not carry out his priestly ministry in an earthly tabernacle (as did the Levitical high priest on the Day of Atonement) but he did in the heavenly sanctuary (vv. 11-12). *Consequently, he has been able to provide unrestricted access to God* (v. 14). *This is the heart of the preacher's argument*. As the core of what he has to say, this paragraph deserves the most careful attention. In 9:11-14 he contrasts the priestly action of Christ with the old Levitical arrangement and outlines the subsequent discussion of 9:15-28.

The frame of reference for the argument in 9:11-14 is clearly the solemn ritual of the Day of Atonement. Within this framework the pastor sets forth a theology of salvation. The procurement of salvation can be described as a forward movement into the presence of God. On the Day of Atonement the high priest sacrificed the bull and the goat in the courtyard of the tabernacle. By carrying the blood in a basin, he would pass through the front compartment into the rear compartment in order to enter the presence of God. In an analogous way, Christ's action on our behalf is described as a forward movement through a front compartment into the awesome presence of God in the real sanctuary in heaven (vv. 11-12). The result of his action is that the limitations of the old covenant have been overcome by the unrepeatable priestly ministry of Christ. *His one offering for sin secured eternal salvation and removed every barrier to the presence of God.*

The ritual of the Day of Atonement offered the preacher a point of comparison with which to describe the significance of the death of Christ in 9:11-14. Christ offered himself as an unblemished sacrifice to God and entered the heavenly sanctuary to complete his priestly ministry in the presence of God (vv. 13-14). *The heavenly liturgy of Christ consists of three movements; namely his death, ascension, and appearance in the presence of God viewed as a unified whole.* The emphasis falls upon Christ whose death was the offering of himself in obedience to God. In short, Christ is both high priest and sacrifice.

This significant unit (9:11-14) is introduced on a note of strong contrast with the description of the Levitical arrangement reviewed in 9:1-10: "But when Christ appeared as high priest of the good things that have now come...he entered once for all into the real sanctuary, thus obtaining eternal redemption" (vv. 11-12a). The preacher balances the presentation of the precedents of redemption in 9:1-10 with the description of redemption itself. The actions described particularly in 9:6-7 are those that preceded the securing of an "eternal redemption," but in 9:11-14 the concern is with an action that obtained eternal redemption. The fact that Christ has been installed as high priest in the heavenly sanctuary indicates that "the time of correction," mentioned in verse 10, has come.

In this description of Christ's priestly action there is *both continuity and discontinuity* with the action of the Levitical high priest on the Day of Atonement. *A single point of continuity is emphasized*: like the Levitical high priest, Christ passed through the front compartment and entered the Most Holy Place by means of blood in order to secure atonement for his people. The accent, however, falls on discontinuity. *Four points of discontinuity are underscored:*

(1)   The location of his priestly ministry was not an earthly tabernacle (cf. 9:1) but the heavenly sanctuary (v. 12*a*).

(2)   The means by which he approached God was not the blood of animals but by means of his own blood (v. 12*b*).

(3)   He was not obligated to enter the Most Holy Place "year by year"; he entered once-for-all (v. 12*a*).

(4)   The result of his priestly action was not the limited recurring cleansing of the annual atonement ritual, but the obtaining of "eternal remption" (v. 12*a*).

The stress falls on Christ's arrival in the heavenly sanctuary and the achievement of eternal redemption. The entrance of Christ into the heavenly sanctuary validates the unique character of his redemptive ministry. *The offer of decisive cleansing may now be extended to the human family through Christ.*

The unusual character of Christ's high priestly achievement is brought out in verses 13-14. The offerings of the Day of Atonement and the sprinkled ashes of a heifer were designed to remove ceremonial defilement. Unfortunately, they left the defiled conscience unaffected. All the sacrifices of the old covenant were able to provide only an external and symbolic removal of defilement. *Their primary importance lay in the witness they bore to the fact that a state of defilement is a hindrance to worship.*

The conception of sin as defilement is a significant emphasis in Hebrews. The contemporary Church has tended to forget this insight. Ironically, whenever the Church neglects a central aspect of the truth, God will jolt the collective memory of his people through the secular world.

A clever TV commercial depicts an attractive cruise director approaching a passenger: "Why Mr. Jones, loosen up your tie. You're on a cruise!" As she adjusts his tie she steps back and blurts out, "Oh, no, Mr. Jones. You've got ring around the collar!" And Mrs. Jones groans, "Oh, those filthy rings!" Then the appeal for the product is made.

Why does an advertisement like that attract our attention? What is there about dirt that finds a response in us? Why does a mother say to a small child going out to play, "Now, don't get dirty"? Why, after a demanding day of hard physical labor and perspiration, do we say, "I feel filthy. I've got to have a shower"?

God has built into our consciousness a sensitivity to the fact of feeling filthy at the surface of our lives as a means of summoning us to recognize that sin makes us dirty within. We have a ten-

dency to forget that fact. Sin corrupts. It is not simply a violation of the law of God; it is a violation of our personhood. Sin
stains us, and demands cleansing. This insight finds a powerful
expression in the familiar lines of William Cowper's hymn:

> There is a fountain filled with blood
> Drawn from Immanuel's veins,
> And sinners plunged beneath the flood
> Lose all their *guilty stains.*
> The dying thief rejoiced to see
> That fountain in his day;
> And there may I, *though vile* as he,
> Wash all my sins away.

Cowper recognized with the writer of Hebrews that sin is not
simply alienation or the expression of a broken relationship. *It is
a reality that stains the sinner and renders him vile. Sin defiles: this
is one aspect of the truth.*

Happily, *there is another aspect of the truth that is stressed* in
Hebrews: *Jesus' blood cleanses us from the defilement of sin* (9:14).
We celebrate this aspect of the truth in confessional hymns:
"What can wash away my sins? Nothing but the blood of Jesus!"
This manner of speaking is not theological language. It is religious language, expressing the response of deep feeling to the experience of redemption. The preacher responsible for Hebrews
understood the power of religious language, and he uses it effectively when referring to the cleansing power of Jesus' blood in
verse 14.

The preacher acknowledges in verse 13 that the old sacrifices
cleansed those who had been ceremonially defiled "to the extent
of the purging of the flesh." This concession calls forth an argument that progresses from the premise of the lesser truth to the
greater truth:

For if the blood of goats and bulls, and the sprinkled ashes of a heifer, sanc-
tify those who have been ceremonially defiled to the extent of the purging of
the flesh, *how much more* will the blood of Christ purge our conscience from
acts that lead to death, so that we may worship the living God! (vv. 13-14).

The reason that Christ is able to achieve what the old sacrifices
could never accomplish is that "he offered himself through the
eternal Spirit as an unblemished sacrifice to God" (v. 14). *The effectiveness of the blood of Christ derives from the qualitatively superior character of his sacrifice.*

The reference to "the blood of Christ" in verse 14 is not to the material substance we refer to as "blood" but to the action of Christ who offered himself to God as an unblemished sacrifice. *The "blood of Christ" is a vivid synonym for the death of Christ in its sacrificial significance.* This understanding of the expression is confirmed when verses 11-14 are summarized in verse 15 in the phrase, "a death having occurred for redemption from transgressions committed under the former covenant."

Christ's death was the sacrifice that inaugurated the new covenant. This is the confident assertion of verse 15 ("And for this reason he is the mediator of a new covenant"). Jesus became the priestly mediator of the new covenant promised in Jer. 31:31-34 because he freely offered his life in obedience to God. His entrance into the heavenly sanctuary confirms God's acceptance of his sacrifice and the ratification of the covenant he mediated.

The penalty for transgressing the old covenant was death. Those who had ratified the covenant had pledged their obedience to the terms of the covenant. But they broke their oath to God. Their sins placed them in jeopardy of being cut off from God. In his death Jesus identified himself with transgressors and took upon himself the curse that was invoked whenever the terms of the covenant were ignored. In an act of supreme obedience *Jesus died a representative death as the cursed one*, so that those he represents may receive the blessings of the covenant promised to those who obey its mandates. Christ's death was a covenant sacrifice.

The reference to Christ's death in verse 15 is followed by a long parenthesis (9:16-22) which explains why it was necessary for Christ to die. The explanation of the death is rooted in covenant practice. The preacher clarifies this matter in verses 16-17:

For where there is a covenant, it is necessary for the death of the one who ratifies it to be brought forward, for a covenant is made legally secure on the basis of the sacrificial victims; it is never valid while the ratifier lives.

These verses explain why Christ had to die in order to become the priestly mediator of the new covenant.

In the Old Testament, ratification of a covenant based on sacrifice frequently called for a procedure which clarifies the detail of verses 16-17. The ratifying party invoked a curse upon himself when he swore to comply with the terms of the covenant. In the transaction the ratifying party was represented by animals designated for sacrifice. The animals would be cut in two, literally.

Then the ratifier would walk between the separated parts of the sacrifice, invoking upon himself a curse if he should fail to be faithful. The bloody dismemberment of representative animals signified the violent death of the ratifying party should he prove faithless to his oath.

An example of this procedure is found in Jeremiah 34:12-20. Israel, under Zedekiah, the king of Judah, broke their covenant with the Lord. In response, God invokes the curse sanction of the covenant. The key section which illustrates the text of Hebrews is as follows:

> The men who have violated my covenant and have not fulfilled the terms of the covenant they made before me, I will treat like the calf they cut in two and then walked between its pieces. The leaders of Judah and Jerusalem, the court officials, the priests and all the people of the land who walked between the pieces of the calf, I will hand over to their enemies who seek their lives. Their dead bodies will become food for the birds of the air and the beasts of the earth (Jer. 34:18-20).

Those who ratified the covenant took a solemn oath to comply with its terms. Walking between the two halves of the calf they had said, "If I do not comply with the terms of this covenant may the Lord do to me, and even more, what I have done with this calf." God now imposes upon faithless Judah the curse sanction of the covenant.

The preacher is familiar with covenant procedure, and he appeals to it to demonstrate that the ratification of the new covenant required the presentation of sacrificial blood. He declares that if a covenant is to be made legally secure, the death of the ratifier must be "brought forward" in a representative sense. Under the old covenant that death was "brought forward" in terms of sacrificial animals. In the case of the new covenant, it was "brought forward" through the death of Christ. Christ became "the cursed one," who in a representative way offered himself on behalf of those who had activated the curse sanction of the old covenant by the transgressions they had committed (see v. 15). He took the curse upon himself. Christ's death was the means of providing the sacrificial blood of the new covenant.

The concern with covenant procedure is sustained in verses 18-21. The preacher demonstrates that the ratification of the old covenant at Sinai under Moses had followed the same procedure. The central thrust of the argument is that *there is an intimate relationship between covenant ratification and sacrificial blood.* The entire argument is summed up in the axiom of verse 22: *defilement is purged by blood.* It is this axiom that provides the basis for comparing the animal sacrifices under the old covenant and the sacrifice of Christ that inaugurated the new covenant. *Without the application of blood there is no definitive putting away of defilement* (v. 22). The reality of the defilement of sin explains why it was necessary for Christ to die a representative death in order to become the priestly mediator of the new covenant.

In the concluding paragraph (9:23-28) the preacher elaborates upon the triumphant announcement in 9:11-12, that Christ has passed through the heavens and has "entered once for all into the real [heavenly] sanctuary, thus obtaining eternal redemption." By his sacrifice and entrance into the heavenly sanctuary Christ purified the sanctuary from the defilement caused by the sins of the people (v. 23). This action corresponds to the purging of defilement from the Most Holy Place, which was the result of the uncleanness and rebellion of Israel on the Day of Atonement (Lev. 16:16). The importance of this thought is developed by means of two contrasts between the action of Christ and the action of the Levitical high priest on the Day of Atonement: (1) The sanctuary Christ entered was not the earthly one, where the Levitical high priest officiated, but heaven itself, the place of God's awesome presence (v. 24). (2) The offering which Christ made was not repeated, unlike the action of the Levitical high priest who year by year entered the Most Holy Place with the sacrificial blood of animals (vv. 25-26). Christ made the single, sufficient sacrifice on the Cross followed by the definitive entrance into the heavenly sanctuary. The result was "the annulling of sin by his sacrifice" (v. 26b). Sin has been put aside; it can no longer accuse or defile. Its ability to call forth a curse has been broken. *Christ's unrepeatable action secured eternal salvation.*

The preacher then offers a fresh perspective on the return of Christ to his people:

And just as it is reserved for men to die once, and after this to experience judgment, so also Christ, after having been offered once to bear the sin of man, will appear a second time to those who are eagerly waiting for him, without reference to sin but for salvation (vv. 27-28).

The reference to Christ's return to those who wait for him draws its force from the analogy with the sequence of events on the Day of Atonement.

On that awesome day the congregation could witness the high

priest entering the sanctuary with a basin of sacrificial blood. They waited anxiously outside the sanctuary while he fulfilled his office within the Most Holy Place. Not until he emerged from the sanctuary was the tension relieved. His return provided assurance that the offering which was made on their behalf had been accepted by God. A sense of the excitement that greeted his reappearance is conveyed by the scribe Joshua ben Sira, who was present in Jerusalem when Simon II the Just, who was high priest in 219-196 BC, officiated on the Day of Atonement:

> How glorious he was when the people gathered round him
>   as he came out of the inner sanctuary!
> Like the morning star among the clouds,
>   like the moon when it is full;
> like the sun shining upon the temple of the Most High,
>   and like the rainbow gleaming in glorious clouds;
> like roses in the days of the first fruits,
>   like lilies by a spring of water,
>   like a green shoot on Lebanon on a summer day;
> like fire and incense in the censer,
>   like a vessel of hammered gold adorned
>   with all kinds of precious stones;
> like an olive tree putting forth its fruit,
>   and like a cypress towering in the clouds
>   (Sirach 50:6-10).

The series of metaphors that seems to run on endlessly are an attempt to express the inexpressible, the excitement, relief, and joy of the people at the return of the high priest after ministering in the sanctuary.

The sequence of entrance into the sanctuary, ministry in the Most Holy Place, and return to the people is reflected in the development of Hebrews 9:24-28. Christ entered the heavenly sanctuary to appear in the presence of God on behalf of his people (v. 24). He will appear "a second time" to those who wait expectantly for him (v. 28). His appearance will confirm that his sacrifice has been accepted and that the force of sin has been decisively broken. The blessings of salvation have been secured for all those whom he represents. For all those who are "the heirs of salvation" (1:14) his return will signal the full enjoyment of their inheritance. As the pastor reflected deeply on the significance of the Day of Atonement he received a distinctly priestly perspective on the return of Christ at the end of this final age.

In summary, the portrayal of the Son of God as our priest in

7:1-28 is complemented in 8:1—9:18 by the teaching that he is also our sacrifice. Christ is both priest and victim. His death is to be understood as a covenant sacrifice which enabled him to ratify the new covenant and to activate its provisions. By the presentation of his life to God as an unblemished offering he overcame the two most serious weaknesses in the old covenantal arrangement; namely severely restricted access to God and the inadequacy of the sacrifice offered to provide decisive cleansing. His fully sufficient sacrifices achieved a decisive removal of sin and won for his people unlimited access to God.

IX

Committed Obedience (Hebrews 10:1-39)

When attempting to concentrate upon the details of the preacher's statement concerning Christ as priest and sacrifice, it is possible to lose sight of the course of the sermon as it unfolds in the great central division of Hebrews. A brief review of the development will restore a sense of perspective concerning the core of the writer's message.

The preacher's initial concern was to bring his friends to a point of emotional readiness for what he had to say concerning Christ as priest and sacrifice (5:11-6:20). He then developed the significant character of Jesus as the high priest like Melchizedek (7:1-25). The superiority of his ministry in the presence of God, and of the new covenant which he ratified, to the old Levitical ministry and the provisions for worship under the old covenant were demonstrated in 8:1—9:10. That demonstration was climaxed by the exposition of the superior character of Christ's one sacrifice, which achieved complete atonement from sin and unrestricted access to the presence of God (9:11-28).

The development to this point is presupposed as the preacher prepares for the final segment of his exposition of Christ's priestly office in 10:1-18. *Once again he directs his attention to the themes of priesthood, sacrifice, and covenant.* The central division of the sermon is finally brought to a conclusion in 10:19-39, when the preacher draws the practical implications for Christian life and worship which follow from the recognition that Jesus is our priest and sacrifice.

In 10:1-18 it will be shown that Jesus is the source of an eternal salvation for those who obey him (5:9). The focus will be on Jesus as the obedient one, and on the response of obedience that

129

is required from his people. Prior to examining the detail of the preacher's statement, it will be helpful to have an overview of what he will say. He develops his thoughts in four paragraphs that are arranged in concentric symmetry:

A   The inadequacy of the provisions of the Law for re-
      peated sacrifices for sins (10:1-4).
B   The repeated sacrifices have been set aside by the one
      sacrifice of Christ who did the will of God (10:5-10).
B'   The Levitical priests have been set aside by the one priest
      enthroned at God's right hand (10:11-14).
A'   The adequacy of the provisions of the new covenant: a
      sacrifice for sins is no longer necessary (10:15-18).

The arrangement is intended to emphasize the correspondence between the first and the fourth paragraphs (A/A'), and between the second and third paragraphs (B/B').

Corresponding to the *inadequacy* of the provisions of the Law for repeated sacrifices for sins is the *adequacy* of the provisions of the new covenant. This sufficiency demonstrates that a sacrifice for sins is no longer necessary. The fourth paragraph shows God's response to the situation described in the first paragraph.

In paragraphs two and three the preacher stresses *a contrast between the many and the one*. In paragraph two, the many sacrifices of the old arrangement were *inadequate*. They have now been set aside by the one sacrifice of Christ, which proved to be *adequate* because he did the will of God. Similarly in paragraph three, the many Levitical priests, whose ministry *never proved to be adequate*, have been replaced by the one priest who is now enthroned in God's presence. His enthronement validates the final and *fully adequate* character of his ministry.

In this final section of the development of Christ's high priestly office, the notions of the inadequacy of the Levitical priesthood and of the sacrifices sanctioned by the Law, and of the adequacy of Christ and his sacrifice are brought before the listeners in a striking manner.

We discover that themes introduced earlier in the sermon are taken up and repeated in 10:1-18. For example, the theme of the enthronement of our high priest at God's right hand was introduced in 8:1; it is repeated in 10:12-13 when the preacher appeals to Psalm 110:1 to show that our high priest has an exalted status. In 8:8-12 the Old Testament passage (Jer. 31:31-34) in which God promised to make a new covenant with his people was cited fully. That text is called to mind when a significant portion of the quotation is cited again in 10:16-17.

There is also a degree of correspondence between the ideas elaborated in 9:1-28 and in 10:1-18. Corresponding to 9:1-10, the section in which the worship provisions of the old covenant are discussed, is the recognition of the ineffectiveness of the repeated sacrifices sanctioned by the law in 10:1-4. The superior achievement of Christ's sacrifice as set forth in 9:11-14 is considered in its historical aspect in 10:5-10. The presentation of the death of Christ as the sacrifice which inaugurated the new covenant in 9:15-28 finds its counterpart in 10:11-18. *These correspondences help us to recognize that the argument developed in 9:1-28 is continued in 10:1-18.*

It is also important to recognize that a fundamental shift in perspective occurs in 10:1-18. In 9:11-28 the preacher was concerned to stress the *"objective" benefits* of Christ's sacrificial offering. *The point of focus was the accomplishment of Christ through his death on the Cross* in terms of his entrance into the heavenly sanctuary in fulfillment of God's eternal plan of salvation. But in 10:1-18 the preacher considers *the "subjective" effects* of Christ's offering on behalf of the community which enjoys the blessings of the new covenant. *Christ's death is considered in terms of its effect upon Christians.*

The thought of 9:11-12 is elaborated in 9:15-28. Emphasis is placed upon the saving work of Christ in relationship to God. We refer to this emphasis as the "objective" character of salvation. The exposition in 9:15-28 clarifies the character of the objective salvation summarized in 9:11-12. The purpose of 10:1-18, however, is to clarify the subjective benefits of salvation surveyed in 9:13-14. There the preacher referred briefly to the decisive cleansing of the conscience of the worshiper, with the consequence that the barrier to the free worship of the living God has been removed. In 9:13-14 the emphasis is placed upon salvation as experienced by Christians. This emphasis is elaborated in 10:1-18. *The focus upon the new situation of the worshiping community, achieved through the effectiveness of Christ's sacrifice, gives to 10:1-18 its distinctive character.*

In this new section the preacher's specific concern is with the purging or cleansing of the conscience. The sacrifices prescribed by the Law were incapable of achieving a decisive cleansing; they could not remove the consciousness of sins. Their ineffectiveness in this regard exposed a basic weakness in the sacrificial provisions of the old covenant. This defect proves that the Law cannot be the actual means of salvation. The preacher writes:

For since the law possesses only a foreshadowing of the good things which were to come, and not the actual form of those realities, it can never decisively purge those who draw near [to God] by the same sacrifices which are offered continuously year after year (10:1).

What follows in verses 2-3 is a parenthetical comment. With the parenthesis, the preacher clarifies the necessity of repeating the same sort of sacrifices every year by appealing to the facts of experience. If these sacrifices had really been effective, all sense of the collective consciousness of defilement would have been removed from the worshipers. As the situation is, however, even on the occasion of the awesome ceremonies associated with the ritual of the Day of Atonement, worshipers continued to experience a "consciousness of sins." *In fact, a sense of the burdened, smiting heart became most pronounced on the Day of Atonement when it was necessary to recognize the transcendent holiness of God.* As long as this sense of sin and transgression with respect to God remained, there could be no effective service of God. The requirement for unhindered access to God is a decisive cleansing of the conscience, and this cleansing has been achieved only through the sacrifice of Christ.

The Day of Atonement was designated as a day for the confession of sins. The elaborate ritual was intended to accentuate a consciousness of sins. The solemn entrance of the high priest into the Most Holy Place dramatized the fact that sin separates the congregation from God. Viewed from this perspective, the sacrifices that were offered actually provided a reminder of the sins which were an obstacle to fellowship with God. *The preacher was impressed that a remembrance of sins was confirmed and renewed year after year by the annual Day of Atonement ritual.*

Once it is understood that verses 2-3 are parenthetical statements, it becomes clear that verse 4 supplies the reason why the sacrifices prescribed by the law were ineffective. The blood of sacrificial animals is insufficient to remove the defilement of sins which constitutes a barrier to worship. The specific reference to "the blood of bulls and goats" shows that the preacher is thinking primarily of the sacrifices prescribed for the Day of Atonement. The sacrifices for that day of fasting and confession were incapable of providing a decisive cleansing.

The establishment of this sober fact demonstrated that the enactment of the new covenant, with its promise that God will not remember sins any longer, was an urgent consideration. This called for the rejection of the many sacrifices prescribed by the law in favor of the one offering of the body of Jesus (10:5-10). It also demanded the rejection of the ineffective ministry of the Levitical priests in favor of the effective ministry of the final priest enthroned in the presence of God (10:11-14). These conclusions encourage us to appreciate the ultimate character of Christ's single personal sacrifice for sins. In this way the preacher establishes a context for defining the blessings of the new covenant which were secured through Jesus' death (10:15-18).

In 10:5-10 the preacher argues that the ineffective sacrifices of the old covenant have been replaced by the sufficient sacrifice of Christ. The arrangements of the Levitical Law, with its annual provision for atonement, have been set aside. The basis for consecrating the new covenant community to the service of God is the unrepeatable offering of the body of Jesus on the cross in fulfillment of the will of God. *Christ came into the world, the preacher asserts, to offer himself to God as an expression of committed obedience.*

Effective use is made of Psalm 40:6-8 in developing this point. In Psalm 40 the writer finds an Old Testament prophecy that God would give greater consideration to a human body as the instrument for accomplishing his will than to the sacrificial offerings prescribed by the law. This prophecy implied the discontinuation of the old arrangements for worship once the new arrangement announced in the psalm had arrived.

The pastor understands the words of Psalm 40:6-8 as the utterance that God's Son spoke to the Father when he entered the world. The passage in Hebrews is descriptive of the incarnation. The eternal Son assumed a human body in order to accomplish the will of God.

> So it is that when Christ comes into the world he says,
> "You did not want sacrifice and offering,
> but you have prepared a body for me.
> You did not like whole burnt offerings
> and sin offerings.
> Then, I said,
> See, I have come
> (it is written about me in the scroll)
> to do your will, O God! (vv. 5-7).

According to this passage, the Christmas story is linked to the accomplishment of the will of God. Jesus is the model of committed obedience to God. He entered the world in fulfillment of the prophetic Scriptures to do the will of God, and to secure for us a relationship with God that is unparalleled in its intimacy.

God's dissatisfaction with the conventional sacrifices can be traced to the fact that *the offering of a sacrifice failed to express a corresponding desire to obey God's will*. This theme is often expressed in prophecy (e.g., 1 Sam. 15:22; Ps. 40:6; 50:8-10; 51:16-17; Isa.1:10-13; 66:2-4; Jer. 7:21-24; Hos. 6:6; Amos 5:21-27). The offering that God finds acceptable represents devotion from the heart. *Sacrifices in themselves are powerless to please God or to secure a proper relationship between God and his people.*

Psalm 40 refers to a speaker who recognized his body as the gift God has prepared so that the divine will may be accomplished. Beyond that reference the preacher recognizes the figure of God's Son who became man in order to fulfill the divine purpose for the human family. *In him intention and the commitment of his body were fully integrated. He accomplished what he came to do.*

The essential utterance of Christ attested by the psalm is the statement, "See, I have come to do your will!" That statement is underscored in verse 9 in order to prepare for the significant conclusion in verse 10: the offering of the body of Christ is the sacrifice God desired to be made. His sacrifice embodied heart-obedience. The fulfillment of the prophecy through Christ's death on Calvary creates a new basis for the consecration of worshipers to the service of God.

The implications of this understanding are overwhelming. God sets aside the repeated sacrifices and the Law which prescribed them. He confirms as valid the link between his will and the effective sacrifice of Christ. In the design of God the fulfillment of Psalm 40:6-8 inaugurates the new arrangement. *The old religious order has been abolished; the new excludes the old*. The first arrangement was suppressed in order to confirm the validity of the new order of relationship (v. 9).

Jesus Christ and the words of Scripture are agents of profound change which introduce a whole new situation for the community of God's people. The hallmark of the new situation is consecration to the service of God on the basis of the totally new offering of the body of Jesus Christ as the inaugural act of the new covenant.

Christ plus nothing

The sacrificial offering of Christ in his death makes explicit the content of the will of God. With the sacrifice of his body on the Cross, Christ freely and fully makes the will of God his own. Consequently, his sacrifice needs no repetition. It embodied the totality of obedience and overcame the disparity between sacrifice and obedience presupposed in Psalm 40:6-8. Christ's self-sacrifice fulfilled the human vocation set forth in the psalm. The fact that he did so under the conditions of authentically human, bodily existence and in solidarity with the human family signifies that he has become the means by which the new people of God have been transformed and consecrated to God's service (v. 10).

The deliberate contrast between the effectiveness of the offerings of the old covenant and the new covenant emphasized in 10:1-10 is sustained in 10:11-14. In this paragraph *the preacher compares the earthly priests who offer sacrifices which are incapable of removing sins, and so must be repeated day by day, and the priest of the new covenant whose sacrificial ministry has been completed.* The comparison is based on the physical posture of the Levitical priests and that of Christ. Every Levitical priest *stands* diligently to perform his priestly duties because his work is never completed. He ministers "day after day" observing the yearly cycle of the daily sacrifices. He offers "the same sacrifices repeatedly" which "can never remove sin utterly" (v. 11). The cumulative effect of the phrases in v. 11 is *a heightened impression of the futility which characterizes the ministry of the Levitical priests.*

Point by point in verses 12-14 the contrast in situation is sharply drawn between the earthly priests and the heavenly priest. The posture of Christ declares the marked difference between him and the Levitical priests. *They stand; he sat down* at the right hand of God when his unique sacrifice was accomplished. Jesus *sits* because his sacrifice requires no repetition. The sacrificial phase of his priestly ministry is completed. Jesus' saving action was accomplished in history, but it possesses a validity which transcends history. The fact that Jesus is seated in the presence of God enables him to exercise in heaven the ministry of the new covenant. No priest of Aaron's line ever sat down in the presence of God in the earthly sanctuary, but Christ has done so in the heavenly sanctuary. *His enthronement in the presence of God attests that the benefits of his sacrificial death endure forever.*

The decisive character of Christ's finished work is affirmed in verse 14: "by one offering he has decisively purged forever those who are being consecrated." *Christ is the one who makes Christians holy.* Consecration signifies that they are being set apart for the service of God. *God's character is pure holiness.* That fact was recognized under the old covenant when the compartment in which God manifested his presence in the tabernacle was called the Holy of Holies or the Most Holy Place. It is recognized under the new covenant when we speak of consecration to the service of God, which is the essence of true worship. *Christ's sacrifice confers on his people a definitive consecration, qualifying them for fellowship with God.*

The preacher finds confirmation of his argument in the witness of the Holy Spirit attested in Scripture (10:15-18). The use of the present tense in verse 15 ("the Holy Spirit also testifies to us") serves to bring the prophetic oracle of Jeremiah 31:33-34 from the past into the present experience of the congregation. The Holy Spirit is speaking *now*. The promise given on the occasion when God first announced his intention to enact a new covenant has *immediate relevance* for the preacher's friends—*and for us.* What was a future expectation in the time of Jeremiah has become a present reality as a result of Christ's death on the Cross. The situation of the Christian community is now prominently in view.

The biblical quotation cited in verses 16-17 serves to relate the preceding discussion of sacrifice and priesthood to the prophecy of the new covenant. The writer interprets the text of Jeremiah in priestly and sacrificial terms because he views the old covenant in these terms. *The finished work of Christ on Calvary was the actual accomplishment of God's intention. The sacrificial arrangement and the prophecy were both pointing towards this fact.* The new covenant arrangement promised through Jeremiah is now the reality of the Christian community.

In the quotation of Jeremiah 31:33-34 *two blessings of the new covenant* are underscored: (1) *God will inscribe his law on the hearts and minds of his people;* (2) *he will no longer remember their sins and misdeeds.* These provisions are the "better promises" of the new covenant to which the preacher alluded in 8:6.

The first blessing indicates that God's people are no longer confronted by an exterior law. The experience of consecration to the service of God, to which reference was made in verses 10 and 14, shows that the promised new relationship to God foretold in the oracle has actually been realized. The reason we can be set apart to serve God out of a heart devotion is that God has inscribed his law upon our hearts.

The second blessing is God's gracious response to the situation of Israel under the old covenant, when the observance of the Day of Atonement amounted to an annual reminder of sins for the covenant people (10:3). The assurance that God will certainly not remember the sins and transgressions of his people under the new covenant is the consequence of the fact that a definitive offering for sins has been made. Christ's atoning death provided the decisive putting away of sins which is presupposed as the basis of Jeremiah's prophecy.

The conclusion to the argument is expressed in an axiom in verse 18: when the sins of God's people have been decisively put away, a sin offering is no longer necessary. The sacrifice offered by Christ on the Cross was the final, sufficient sacrifice for sins for all those who acknowledge Jesus Christ as their Savior. The fact that Christ entered the world to do the will of God (10:5-7) shows that *he was the one person in whom the intention of the new covenant was achieved completely. His adherence to the will of God, even in death, indicates that God had inscribed his laws on the human heart.*

Sins no longer provide an obstacle to an enduring covenantal relationship to God. The people of the new covenant enjoy through Christ unhindered access to God in worship. *The only sacrifice required of them is the sacrifice of praise* (13:15).

The task of the Christian community is to appropriate the truth as set forth in 8:1—10:18 and to respond to it with obedience. This is made clear in 10:19-39, a section in which the preacher applies to the situation of his friends what he has developed in the core of his sermon.

The transition from the careful presentation of God's Son as our priest and sacrifice to the response required of Christians is accomplished sharply in verses 19-25. What the pastor says to his friends can be grasped if we simplify his statement to its bare minimum:

Since we have authorization for free access to the heavenly sanctuary by means of the blood of Jesus...and *since we have* a great priest... *Let us* continue to draw near to God with a sincere heart in fullness of faith.... *Let us* continue to hold fast the hope we profess.... *Let us* keep on caring for one another for the stimulation of love and good works, *not* discontinuing our meeting together... *but* rather encouraging one another.

Here we have a turning point in the sermon. This is the climax to which the preacher has been leading his friends. Here he summarizes what is said about Christ as our priest and sacrifice in order to summon his friends to apply the blessings of Christ's high priestly ministry to their lives.

As a section the four paragraphs of 10:19-39 display *a familiar sequence.* It is familiar because it was introduced to the members of the house church in 5:11—6:12. The structural parallel between these two sections can be exhibited in a table.

5:11-6:12			**10:10-39**
A	5:11—6:3	Reminder of the actual situation of the community.	A' 10:19-25
B	6:4-8	Warning against apostasy.	B' 10:26-31
C	6:9-10	Encouragement based on past performance.	C' 10:32-34
D	6:11-12	Appeal focused on the future.	D' 10:35-39

There is an undeniable formal resemblance between 5:11—6:12 and 10:19-39.

The formal resemblance between these two sections of the sermon, however, should not obscure the fact that each is distinct in content and purpose: 5:11—6:12 prepares the writer's friends to receive the teaching elaborated in 7:1—10:18; 10:19-39 applies that teaching to the situation addressed in the sermon. This new unit draws upon that teaching, especially the development in 8:1—10:18, as a source of motivation for the house-church. This is evident, for example in verses 19-21, 26, and 29, where the formulation of the writer's statement is richly informed by the teaching in 9:11—10:18:

Therefore, brothers and sisters, since we have authorization for free access to the heavenly sanctuary by means of the blood of Jesus, a way which is new and which leads to life, which he made available for us through the curtain, (that is to say, by means of his flesh), and since we have a great priest in charge of God's household (vv. 19-21; see 9:11-28).

For if we deliberately persist in sin after we have received the full knowledge of the truth, there is no longer any sacrifice for sins (v. 26; see 9:14, 24-28; 10:12-14).

How much severe punishment do you suppose will he deserve who has tram-
pled upon the Son of God and who has treated the blood of the covenant, by
which he was consecrated, as defiled (v. 29; see 9:15-22; 10:10, 14).

The clear references to the teaching presented in the central division of the sermon where the preacher developed the heart of his
message sheds light on the note of urgency in the appeal expressed in these closing verses to "draw near to God." *The appeal
looks at the Christian life as worship—as a continual approach to the
living God.*
 The background to what the preacher has to say in verses 19-
25 is found in the peace, or the fellowship, offering. Previous to
this point in the sermon, the high-priestly work of Christ has
been presented against the background of the Day of Atonement
and the sin offering (cf. 9:6-7, 11-14, 24-28). The sin offering is a
wholly burnt offering. Although the blood of the sacrifice was
collected in a basin and was taken by the high priest into the
Most Holy Place for application to the altar of judgment, the
body of the slain animal was taken outside the camp where it
was burned (cf. 13:11-12).
 It is Christ, the sin offering which provides us with access to
God, who allows us to consider the Christian life as worship. Yet
the preacher's friends had failed to grasp the implications for fellowship and worship which follow naturally from the life and
death of Jesus. That is evident in verse 25, where the writer must
sadly acknowledge that some members of the house-church had
stopped attending the worship services altogether. *Christian worship is expected from the new people of God because God has restored
them to a relationship characterized by peace through Christ, the
perfect sacrifice for sins.*
 In the argument developed in chapters 9-10 there is a focus on
the ratification of the new covenant (9:15-21; 10:16-17). Covenant ratification necessarily involves a peace offering to signify
the acceptance of the terms of the covenant by the participants.
This was the case, for example, in the ratification of the covenant
God made with Israel at Sinai (Exod. 20:24). The peace-offering
sealed the covenant. The fellowship meal, which was the characteristic feature of the peace offering, displayed the peaceful relationship of the participants.
 In any series of offerings, the peace offering is mentioned last
because it cannot be presented until sin has been atoned and the
broken relationship mended. The preacher moves from the

thought of accomplishing atonement (9:11—10:14) to that of the act of ratifying a covenant, (10:15-18) to a discussion of worship (10:19-25), because sins have been decisively atoned by Christ.

The character of the peace, or fellowship offering is defined in Leviticus 3:1-17 and 7:11-34. In this offering the blood of the sacrifice was caught in a basin and was sprinkled on the altar to symbolize atonement, but the body of the animal was roasted on the altar as a fragrant sacrifice to the Lord, and then it was shared with the worshipers at a fellowship meal. It was understood that the meal was hosted by God. The meal symbolized the intimacy of the fellowship with the Lord. It became an occasion for the public recital of God's covenant faithfulness (Psalm 26:4-7; 116:12-19). The peace offering could focus upon thanksgiving (Lev. 7:11, 12, 15) or upon the dedication of the worshiper to the service of God (Lev. 7:16-17; 22:21). It was thus an offering that was particularly suited to stress the reality of consecration to God.

Once this background is appreciated, it becomes clear that the exhortations in verses 22-25 rest upon a pattern of worship that reflects the ancient peace offering.

(1) *The congregation gathers for mutual exhortation to faith (v. 22), hope (v. 23), and love (v. 24).* That the thought of an offering lies behind these verses is suggested by the introductory words in verse 22, "let us continue to *draw near to God."* The same formulation was actually used in 10:1 in reference to those who drew near to God under the old covenant by means of the sacrificial offerings which were repeated every year on the Day of Atonement. In the Old Testament the invitation, "Let us draw near to God," is used when encouraging believers to approach God's presence to receive instruction or to enter into worship. In the context of verse 22, "to draw near" is to render acceptable worship in the heavenly sanctuary as those who have been consecrated to the service of God by Jesus' blood (see vv. 19-21).

(2) *The peace offering in the Old Testament is an occasion for the public recital of God's covenant faithfulness.* So in verse 23 we find an allusion to the public act of declaring the goodness of God and his covenant love. The reference to unwavering commitment calls to mind the vow of allegiance that was commonly made on the occasion of the peace offering. The vow was to be fulfilled in the presence of those who were gathered to share the fellowship meal.

(3) *It is characteristic of the peace offering that it can never be*

made alone. This fact sheds light on the emphases in verses 24-25:

And let us keep on caring for one another for the stimulation of love and good works, not discontinuing our meeting together as some people are regularly doing, but rather encouraging one another, and all the more since you see the Day of the Lord approaching.

God's promises and blessings are to be recounted in the fellowship gathering for the purpose of stimulating faith, hope, and love. That is why we ought to gather together for worship (v. 25). *Although faith and hope can be exercised by the individual Christian, the expression of love is possible only in community.* Distinctively Christian qualities of life are to be developed *in fellowship* on the basis of the peaceful relationship established between God and his people.

The distinctive appreciation of the importance of worship in Hebrews, where the writer draws upon the tradition of the ancient peace offering, provides a fresh perspective for the celebration of thanksgiving and the sharing of a fellowship meal. We gather together to express thanks to the covenanting Lord and for mutual encouragement to faith, hope, and love.

The disloyalty of some members of the house-church, who had deserted the community (v. 25), explains the sternness of the warning that follows in 10:26-31. Worship and mutual encouragement are the responsibility of those who have enjoyed the blessings of the new covenant. The neglect of the gatherings of the assembly displayed a contemptuous disregard for the benefits of Christ's sacrifice and exposed those careless Christians to severe judgment.

The strong warning in verses 26-31 is parallel in statement to 6:4-8. Like that earlier passage, it exposes the grave peril of the sin of apostasy. The situation which can result in inexorable judgment is reviewed in four aspects:

(1)   *the experience of Christian reality* ("after we have received the full knowledge of the truth," v. 26);

(2)   *the fact of apostasy* ("If we delibertately persist in sin," v. 26. The actual character of the sin is clarified in v. 29);

(3)   *the recognition that renewal is impossible* ("there is no longer any sacrifice for sin," v. 26).

(4)   *the imposing of the curse sanctions of the new covenant* ("only an inevitable terrifying expectation of judgment and of raging fire ready to consume God's adversaries," v. 27).

The sin of apostasy entails irreversible consequences.

The measure of privilege that distinguishes the people of the new covenant from those who lived under the conditions of the old covenant (cf. 8:6-13; 10:15-18) necessarily defines the extent of the peril placed upon those who despise the benefits of the new covenant. They not only forfeit the blessings of the new covenant but they experience the profound religious dread of those who anticipate the judgment of God because they have disparaged Christ's covenant sacrifice (vv. 29-31).

The reference to apostasy in verses 26-31 is related to the preacher's concern for worship as the appropriate response to the enactment of the new covenant. A scornful disdain for Christ and a rejection of the adequacy of his sacrifice creates an inability to worship God. *There can be no true worship of God apart from the sufficient sacrifice of Christ.* The apostate, who has spurned the sacrifice of Christ, cannot be readmitted to the worshiping community because he cannot satisfy the conditions for worship. *Ironically, the alternative to worship is apostasy.*

It probably was the experience of suffering, abuse, loss, and disappointment in the world that accounts for the desertion of the community acknowledged in verse 25. Christians must not be subverted by a form of worldliness which would ultimately separate them from Christ and from each other. The preacher seeks to counter this dangerous development by reminding the congregation of their courageous stand in the past, when they exhibited a bold commitment to Christ and to each other in spite of suffering and adversity (vv. 32-35). The remembrance of their past performance provides a powerful incentive for continuing boldness and loyalty to Christ in the present and for the future.

Certainty and stability ought to characterize a Christian presence in the world. The ultimate source of such qualities of life is the utter reliability of God. He has acknowledged his firm commitment to the community in the provisions of the new covenant and through his binding word of promise (vv. 23, 36). The constancy of God guarantees that the response of faithfulness cannot be in vain. It will result in "the acquisition of life" (v. 39). The exhortation to steadfast endurance and to faithfulness extended to the preacher's friends in verses 36-39 is precisely a reminder of that fact. It constitutes an appeal for fidelity which is focused upon the future.

In summary, Christ came into the world in order to model committed obedience to the will of God. As the obedient one, he came to do the will of God. The sacrifice of his body on the Cross was the obedient response to the divine will, and this sacrifice secured for his people the benefits of the new covenant. His sacrifice conferred upon the new people of God a definitive consecration to the service of God, which is the essence of true worship. As a direct result of the blessings secured through the committed obedience of Christ, we are enabled to be the people who also demonstrate committed obedience. We prove that we are the new people of God precisely as the obedience which Christ displayed when he entered the world becomes the hallmark of our lives.

It is clear that 10:1-39 elaborates the preacher's earlier declaration that Christ, having been qualified to come before God in priestly action, became the source of an eternal salvation to those who obey him (5:9). The preacher calls his friends to identify themselves as the heirs of salvation by committed obedience in response to the priestly achievement of Christ.

X

Committed Faith
(Hebrews 11:1—12:3)

Text

The men and women for whom Hebrews was prepared were facing an uncertain future. The writer responsible for the sermon was a man with a pastor's heart who regarded these people as friends. He wanted to encourage them to be faithful to Christ at a time when discipleship could be costly. He knew that they were tempted to forget the extent of their privilege and the richness of their experience as Christians. He offered them the encouragement that they possessed through Christ the blessings of the new covenant. Moreover, they were the heirs to the utterly reliable promise of God. In the priestly ministry of Christ and the constancy of God, they possessed sufficient resources to sustain them in a period characterized by peril and persecution.

The preacher holds before his friends their own example of steadfast commitment to Christ under adverse circumstances in the past in order to encourage the same courageous stance in the present:

Remember those earlier days, after you received the light, when you endured a hard contest with sufferings. Sometimes you were publicly exposed to ridicule, both by insults and persecutions, and on other occasions you showed solidarity with those who were treated in this way, for in fact you shared the suffering of those in prison, and cheerfully accepted the seizure of your property, because you knew you yourselves had better and permanent possessions. Therefore, do not throw away your boldness, seeing that it has a great reward (10:32-35).

They had been loyal to Jesus in difficult circumstances.

The key to appreciating the circumstances to which the writer alludes is provided in the statement, "you cheerfully accepted the seizure of your property" (10:34). The reference to the seizure or confiscation of property suggests a people who were subject to a decree of expulsion. Those who were expelled or banished found that their property was defenseless. It is natural to recall the reference to the expulsion of certain Jewish leaders from Rome under Claudius in the year AD 49 (see Suetonius, *Life of the Deified Claudius* 25:4, discussed above, pp.22-23).

The decree of expulsion was the result of social disturbances in the Jewish quarters in reaction to the conviction that Jesus was the promised Messiah. Among those who were expelled from Rome were the Jewish Christian leaders, Aquila and Priscilla, whom Paul met in Corinth (Acts 18:1-2). There is a high degree of probability that the men and women who made up this house-church had shared the hardships of that period of disruption. They had experienced abuse, imprisonment, and the loss of their property. The friends of the preacher had demonstrated courage and loyalty to Christ under trying circumstances.

With the lifting of the decree they had returned to Rome and had again become property owners (cf. Rom. 16:3-5). Life had become settled and comfortable. But then in AD 64 persecution broke out once more. This time it was more vehement. Under Claudius there had been imprisonment and banishment; under Nero there were executions (Tacitus, *Annals of Rome*, 15:44). The men and women of the house-church suddenly found themselves weary with the necessity of sustaining the high level of commitment they had brought to Christ in those earlier days.

Time and fear appear to have eroded Christian commitment. *Then* they had been bold for Jesus Christ; *now* they appear to have become timid. *Then* they had stood their ground; *now* they appear to be in retreat. *Then* they had regarded their property as expendable; *now* they are emotionally unprepared to risk the loss of property and of life. That is why the preacher reminds his friends of their former witness and urges them not to throw away their boldness, adding, "seeing that it has a great reward" (10:35). He means, of course, that sustained and committed boldness will be richly rewarded by God.

In 10:36-39 the preacher spoke directly to their need: "You need, then, endurance so that after you have done the will of God you may receive the promise" (10:36). That note was sounded in the sermon as early as 6:11: " We want each one of you to show the same earnest concern with regard to the realization of your hope until the end." *Endurance* is the demonstration to the very end of the course, of earnest concern for the enjoyment of all that has been promised in Christ. "You need, then, endurance so that after you have done the will of God you may receive the promise" (10:36).

The will of God for this early Christian community was the display of courage and firm Christian commitment in the hostile environment of imperial Rome. It is the exhibition of the quality of life which Christ makes possible in a decaying and dying world. The will of God is that Christians should experience the privilege of access to God and a clean conscience, which make it possible to find in God an impenetrable refuge when they are subject to attack and humiliation.

The preacher assures his friends that when they have done the will of God they will receive what he has promised. What God has promised is that Christ will return as the glorified and exalted Judge who will vindicate his people and validate their faith in him: "A little while longer, the Coming One will come; he will not delay" (10:37). This citation from Habakkuk 2:3 affirms that the Lord will surely return. In fact, the next event on God's timetable for the salvation of his people is the return of Christ as Judge. "The Coming One" is Jesus. He "will come; he will not delay." *Christian courage is holding on a moment longer while we wait for the advent of Christ.*

The declaration concerning the Coming One in Habakkuk is followed by the statements that are quoted in 10:38: "But my righteous one will live by faithfulness. But if he draws back I myself will reject him" In this context, it is clear that God's "righteous one" who will live by faith is the committed Christian, whose faith resides in the objective content of God's word of promise. God has promised that "the Coming One will come," and the man and woman of faith responds, "I will live in the light of that coming. I will respond to my circumstances knowing that God's word of promise is utterly reliable. I will identify myself with God and with the content of his promise."

The Christian makes this response because he desires to please God and because he wants God to be pleased with him. He knows that God has said, "But if he draws back, I will not be pleased with him" (10:38b). God is gathering a company of committed men, women, and young adults who will be consistent in their relationship with him. These are the people of the new covenant who are in a position to delight the Lord. *They please him!*

The biblical quotation from Habakkuk 2:3-4 sets before the

community of faith two options: Christians can live by faith and please the Lord, or they can turn away and displease him. That was the sharp alternative the preacher brings to the attention of his friends, only to respond for them: "But we are not of those who draw back, leading to destruction, but of those who are faithful, culminating in the acquisition of life" (10:39). *Ruin or vindication, destruction or salvation, death or life are the options of the Christian community as it is called every day to responsible commitment.* That explains why the preacher immediately directs the attention of his friends to the demand for committed faith in 11:1—12:3.

The recommendation and celebration of faith in 11:1-40 is firmly attached to the context. Knowing that some members of the house-church had deserted the community (10:25) and that among those who remained there appeared to be a loss of confidence in the promise of God (10:35), the preacher had stressed the utter reliability of God. His faithfulness to his promise guarantees that the reward for doing the will of God will be reception of what he has promised (10:23, 36). The will of God, however, is defined by the prophetic oracle, "My righteous one will live by faith" (10:38). The context gives to the concept of "faith" the sense of steadfast faithfulness to God and to his word of promise. The identification of Christians as those who have faith and so acquire life (10:39) invited clarification of the dynamic character of committed faith.

In 11:1-40 faith is shown to be a quality of response to God which celebrates the reality of promised blessings and the objective certainty of events announced but as yet unseen (11:1). This understanding is substantiated by a catalogue of persons and events which the preacher views from the perspective of *faith in action*. The demonstration of the effective power of faith under the old covenant verifies the character and possibilities of faith for the Christian community.

Earlier in the sermon the pastor counseled his friends to imitate "those who with faith and steadfast endurance inherit the promises" (6:12), and he cited Abraham as an example for his friends (6:13-15). That unit anticipated the catalogue of approved witnesses to committed faith in 11:1-40. In that earlier passage, as here, the emphasis is placed *on the life of faith as a believing response to the promise of God.* The preacher's thoughts move entirely on the plane of history. He brings before his friends a long list of exemplary witnesses to an enduring faith, and he demonstrates *that faith is essentially determined by hope.* The list of persons and events from Israel's past shows that throughout the history of salvation approval from God has been based upon the evidence of a living faith which acts in terms of God's promises, even when the realization of the promise is not in sight. Such a dynamic faith is able to move beyond disappointments and the sufferings experienced in this world and to bear a ringing testimony to future generations of the reality in the promised blessings.

The new section opens with a triumphant affirmation concerning the character of faith and a brief summary of the catalogue of examples which is to follow:

Now faith celebrates the objective reality of the blessings for which we hope, the demonstration of events as yet unseen. On this account the men and women of the past received approval by God (11:1-2).

The series of events and persons selected from the pages of the Scripture, and presented in chronological sequence in verses 3-31, is elaborated in terms of the characterization of *faith* in verse 1 and its sequel, verse 6: "And without faith it is impossible to please God, for it is necessary for the person approaching God to believe that he exists and that he becomes a rewarder of those who seek him out." These first paragraphs move selectively and rapidly through Genesis 1 to Joshua 6.

The writer then alters the format of his presentation in verse 32. He renounces any further attempt to list one by one the exemplary persons and events of the Scripture and contents himself with a summarizing catalogue. A simple enumeration of the names of those who through faith experienced triumph or deliverance from certain death (vv. 32-35*a*) prepares for the frank acknowledgment of unnamed men and women of faith who were not delivered from hardship, suffering, and death (vv. 35*b*-38). The section is then rounded off with a summarizing conclusion which serves to relate the experience of those who lived faithfully in terms of the promise of God under the old covenant to those who are Christians (vv. 39-40).

The structure of the development can be exhibited in an outline.

(A)   The celebration of faith (11:1-2).
(B)   The role of faith (11:3-38).
    (1)   Creation to Noah (vv. 3-7).

    (2)   The patriarchs (vv. 8-22).
    (3)   Moses to the conquest of Jericho (vv. 23-31).
    (4)   Triumphs over opposing powers (vv. 32-35*a*).
    (5)   Sufferings in life and death (vv. 35*b*-38).
  (C) The importance of faith   (11:39-40).

The opening declaration of the section (11:1) is not intended to be a formal definition of faith. It is instead a recommendation and celebration of the faith that results in the acquiring of true life (10:39). As a statement that sums up all that the preacher wanted to affirm about the intensity and capacity of faith, it is confessional in character. It concentrates in a single, compact sentence the theme and interpretation that the following examples will illustrate: "Now faith celebrates the objective reality of the blessings for which we hope, the demonstration of events as yet unseen." Every word has been carefully chosen and weighed for its significance in order to draw attention to the characteristics of faith which were especially relevant to the preacher's friends in their situation.

The object that faith celebrates is considered under two aspects: (1) "the reality of the blessings for which we hope"; (2) "the demonstration of events as yet unseen." The meaning of the first of these expressions can be brought out by resorting to paraphrase: faith celebrates *now* the reality of the future blessings which make up the objective, or actual, content of Christian hope. Faith gives to the objects of hope the force of present realities, and it enables the person of faith to enjoy the full certainty that in the future these realities will be experienced. Faith provides the objective ground upon which Christians may base their subjective confidence. *It is this capacity of faith that allows Christians to maintain a firm grasp upon truth which cannot be demonstrated, and to display quietness in the presence of hostility, in the knowledge that the blessings for which they hope are guaranteed by the promise of God.*

The meaning of the second of these expressions is equally daring: faith demonstrates the existence of reality which cannot be grasped through our senses. Faith confers upon spiritual reality that we cannot see the full certainty of a *proof* or a *demonstration*; it furnishes *evidence* concerning that which has not been seen. *Christians know that realities which are not seen now will be seen in the future.* In that sense, faith is the demonstration of the substantial reality of events as yet unseen.

This kind of faith is an effective power which is directed toward the future. Its source is a direct, personal encounter with the living God. The forward-looking capacity of faith enables a person to advance courageously and confidently into an unseen future, supported only by the word of God. Committed faith is a positive orientation of life toward God and his word. Consequently, faith has the ability to unveil the future so that the solid reality of events as yet unseen can be appreciated by believers. The men and women, to whom the pastor refers in the list of approved witnesses which follows 11:1, all directed the effective power of faith to realities which for them lay in the future (11:7, 10, 13, 27, 31, 35-38). They were not dismayed by harsh circumstances. They found in faith a reliable guide to the future.

It should be evident immediately that this is a different approach to faith than the perspective expressed by the apostle Paul in his letters. *For Paul, faith is our subjective response to what God has done in the past.* Faith looks back to Christ's death on Calvary and affirms, "That death was for me." Faith may be described as a backward glance that releases us to act responsibly as Christians in the present. *In Hebrews, however, faith is focused upon the future. It has an objective character* because it is tied to the promise of God. Faith celebrates "the objective reality" or "demonstration" that what God has promised will be realized. *It is the proof that God's redeeming love surrounds us and sustains us.*

In short, we should think of faith in Hebrews in two ways: (1) *Faith is an openness to the future* which expresses itself now through obedient trust in the God who has spoken through a word of promise. (2) *Faith is a present grasp on invisible truth expressed through the promise of God.* Committed faith looks to the future, and it acts in the present in the light of that future. The future is certain because it is guaranteed by the promise of the God who cannot lie. Committed faith finds expression as a persevering faithfulness to God (11:6).

This double perspective on faith is underscored by the verbs. The emphasis falls on *the capacity for understanding, remembering, and seeing that faith made possible*:

By faith *we understand* that the universe was ordered by the word of God, so that what is seen was not brought into being from anything observable (v. 3).
By faith *Joseph*, while coming to the end of his life, *remembered* God's promise of an exodus from Egypt, and gave instructions concerning the burial of his bones (v. 22).

In accordance with the principle of faith, all these persons died, not having received the fulfillment of the promises, but only *seeing* them and saluting them from a distance (v. 13).

[Moses] regarded abuse incurred for the sake of the Christ greater wealth than the treasures of Egypt, because he was *looking ahead* to the reward. By faith he left Egypt, not fearing the king's rage, for *he kept* the who is invisible *continually before his eyes*, as it were (vv. 26-27).

In each of these passages the character of faith as a present grasp on invisible truth or as openness to the future expressed through obedient trust in God's reliable word of promise is evident in the formulation.

This was the expression of committed faith for which men and women in Israel's history were commended by God. They are the approved witnesses who can be paraded before us as models of faithfulness to God in difficult and uncertain circumstances. The faith which is celebrated in 11:4-38 is characterized by firm reliability and steadfastness. It is unwavering trust in God and in his promises (vv. 6, 17-19, 22, 29). The context shows that these attested witnesses affirm the reliability of God, who is faithful to his promise (v. 11). *Committing themselves to God who is steadfast, these examples of faith in action were themselves made steadfast.*

This concept of faith is rooted in the Old Testament, where faith and hope are closely allied. The relationship between faith and the realization of the promise of God, which is stressed throughout this section of the sermon, shows that it is the property of faith to make hope secure (vv. 1, 9, 10, 13, 24-26, 39).

A closer look at Abraham in verses 8-10 (which characterizes verses 4-31) focuses upon his departure from the city in which he was born—the ancient city of Ur on the Euphrates River in which he had spent most of his mature life—and his subsequent life as a wandering nomad in Mesopotamia and Canaan.

Abraham, at the age of seventy-five years, left familiar surroundings in response to the call of God, even though he did not know where he was going. He engaged in a journey, and *the journey became a parable of the character of the life of committed faith*.

The preacher selected the example of Abraham because his experiences exposed the qualities of godly life. He asks his friends to consider godly life under three of its aspects.

(1) *Godly life is the response of committed faith to the call of God* ["by faith Abraham, as he was being called obeyed by departing" (v. 8)] A strong sense of the call of God has been characteristic of

men and women of faith throughout the history of revelation. *Faith coming to expression as obedience is the appropriate response to that call.* Abraham had a high election-consciousness; he knew that the hand of God was upon his life; guiding him, directing him, sustaining him. The preacher stresses the immediateness of Abraham's response to the call of God: "as he was being called he obeyed by departing." The clause, "he set out not knowing where he was going," indicates that the details were unclear to Abraham but the fact of God's direction was an indelible impression. It is important to appreciate the risk this actually was for Abraham.

In the office occupied by the distinguished Australian churchman, Stuart Barton Babbage, there hung four photographs of open desert. The fact that the four photographs were virtually identical aroused my curiosity. I had to ask why he had displayed them side by side. He replied that he had visited ancient Ur. While on the site of the ruins he had aimed his camera toward the north, the east, the south, and the west, in each direction snapping a picture. Whether one looked to the north or to the east, to the south, or to the west, beyond the walls of Ur there was only a bleak prospect. Ur was a great city with a high standard of civilization. It was a fertile place, watered annually by the flooding of the Euphrates. But beyond the city walls was simply empty terrain. Yet Abraham obeyed God's call by departing from Ur. His obedience was the response of committed faith.

— (2) *Godly life is the response of committed faith to an alien environment* ["by faith he migrated to the promised land as to a foreign land" (v. 9)]. Abraham in Canaan was like a stranger in a strange land. His dress, his appearance, his mannerisms, his accent permitted everyone to recognize that he was an alien in the land. The implication of the preacher's statement is that Abraham's life-style, his values, and his goals were determined not by his surroundings but by the vision of God and an unwavering conviction that God had called him through a word of promise.

The promised land to which he emigrated was like a foreign country, in which he lived a nomadic existence. The detail that he, together with his son Isaac and his grandson Jacob, lived in tents implies that he had not come to settle down, to establish roots in a culture devoid of God. He was on pilgrimage as an expression of committed faith.

— (3) *Godly life is the response of committed faith to the promise of God* ["for he was looking forward with certainty to the city which has foundations because its designer and creator is God"

(v. 10)]. Abraham left one city for another. He exchanged a life of settled comfort in a major urban center for an existence marked by privation and wandering in pursuit of the promise of God. The note of anticipation which is a hallmark of the godly life is well expressed in the clause, "he was looking forward with certainty to the city which has foundations." *Anticipation invites preparation*, and all of his anticipation was focused upon arrival in a city where the unsettled existence of a nomad would be exchanged for life in a city with immovable foundations. The goal of his migration was the City of God. The motivation for the disruption that pilgrimage always entails is participation in the kingdom of God.

The statement that Abraham was looking forward with certainty to the City of God is an important corrective to the declaration in verse 8 that he did not know where he was going. He possessed a sure sense of direction; he would go wherever he felt God leading him. He did not suffer from a lack of vision for the future.

This is a remarkable perspective from which to respond to the hardening of attitudes toward the life of faith. In many persons there is found little or no interest in spiritual reality. They express a basic satisfaction with day-to-day routine, but exhibit no concern for where they are going. They have *no goals*; they display *no striving*; they appear to be motivated by *no dreams*. They suffer from what can be labeled as "destination sickness." They have no defined destination; they are merely drifting. Abraham did not suffer from destination sickness.

The striking conclusion to this unit is found in verses 13-16, where the preacher looks back upon the experience of the patriarchs Abraham, Isaac, and Jacob:

In accordance with the principle of faith all these persons died, not having received the fulfillment of the promises, but only seeing them and saluting them from a distance, and confessing that they were strangers and sojourners in the land. Now people who say such things show plainly that they are expecting intently a homeland of their own. If they had meant that country from which they had set out, they would have had opportunity to return. But as it is they were longing for a better homeland, in other words, a heavenly one, for which reason God is not ashamed to be called their God, for he has made ready a city for them.

The concluding statements confirm that *God is committed to those who respond to him through committed faith*.

The example of Abraham illustrates the character of committed faith. Faith is openness to the future which expresses itself now through obedient trust in God who has spoken through a word of promise. It is this aspect of faith that clarifies the immediateness with which Abraham acted upon the call of God to exchange the familiar surroundings of Ur for a nomadic existence in Mesopotamia, Canaan, and Egypt. Like the other witnesses to follow, *he demonstrated an openness to the future guaranteed only by the promise of God.*

Faith is also *a present grasp upon invisible truth* expressed through the promise. It is this aspect of faith which clarifies how Abraham knew that the ultimate fulfillment of the promise was the City of God. As an approved model of faithfulness, he is a witness to Christians concerning the reality of the promised City of God. That promise belongs to the people of God today as certainly as it belonged to the patriarch Abraham.

It is clear that verses 8-19 are not simply a summary of Abraham's life, character, and faith. They provide for the preacher's friends a brief history of the promise of God considered in terms of Abraham's call and migration to Canaan (vv. 8-10), the conception of Isaac (vv. 11-12), the deferring of the fulfillment of the promise (vv. 13-16), and the command to sacrifice Isaac (vv. 17-19). The manner in which the material is developed indicates that *the exemplary conduct of Abraham is informative precisely because it sheds light on the content of Christian faith.* The yearning of the patriarchs for a homeland of their own is a witness to the Christian community of the reality of a heavenly homeland (vv. 14-16).

The models of committed faith reviewed in verses 4-31 cover the witness of Scripture from Genesis to Joshua 6. It seems as if the preacher suddenly realized that he could not continue his catalogue of witnesses to the life of committed faith under the old covenant; there was simply too much to tell: "And what more shall I say? For time would fail me if I tell about Gideon, Barak, Samson, Jephthah, of both David and Samuel and the prophets" (v. 32). In the verses that follow he paints with broad strokes on the canvas of redemptive history to focus briefly on the achievements of faithful men and women who responded to God with committed faith:

who through faith conquered kingdoms [Gideon, Barak, Samson, Jephthah, and David], practiced justice, and attained the promised blessings [Samuel and the prophets], who shut the mouths of lions [Daniel], extinguished the

fury of the flames [Shadrach, Meshach, Abednego], and escaped the edge of
the sword [David and the prophets] who after weakness became strong
[Samson, Esther]; who became mighty in war and routed foreign armies [Gideon, Barak, Jephthah, David, Samuel]. Women received their dead by resurrection [the widow of Zarepheth of Sidon, the Shunammite woman] (vv.
33-35a).

The summary surveys those who enjoyed the rich benefits of
committed faith after difficult trials.

The catalogue then gives place to a recital of the experience of
others, for whom deliverance came only through suffering and
martyrdom. It was imperative to acknowledge to the members of
the house-church that the possession of triumphant faith did not
necessarily imply an immunity from persecution, humiliation,
and violent death:

But others were tortured, after refusing to accept the offered release in order
that they might attain a better resurrection. And others experienced jeering
and lashing, and even chains and prison. They were stoned; they were sawn
in two; they were murdered by the sword. They went about in sheepskins
and goatskins, destitute, oppressed, mistreated (humanity was not worthy
of them). They wandered aimlessly in uninhabited regions and on mountains, and in caves and crevices in the ground (vv. 35b-38).

The reference to men and women of committed faith who were
not rescued by God demonstrates that *faith also stands in narrow
association with endurance.* There is a sharp contrast between the
triumphant affirmation of verse 34 ("they escaped the edge of the
sword") and the sober acknowledgment of verse 37 ("they were
murdered with the sword"). Although these heroic individuals
were not delivered from humiliation and death they remained
faithful. *They demonstrated firm persevering faithfulness.*

The experiences surveyed in verses 35b-38 were those which
could become the sufferings of the preacher's friends—jeers,
flogging, pursuit, and death. They presuppose a commitment
which lays hold of God in the furnace of affliction precisely
when there is no indication that God will break through and rescue his people in some miraculous manner. When tormentors
taunt, "Where is your God?" men and women of committed faith
respond, "I will place my trust in him!"

The importance of faith, and of the life of committed faith, is
underscored in the closing verses of this section, where the pastor
summarizes what he has been demonstrating:

And although they all had received approval from God through faith, they did not receive what had been promised. God had provided something better with us in mind, so that they should not reach perfection without us (vv. 39-40).

The new feature in these verses is the focus upon the relevance for the Christian community of the recital of the approved witnesses of faith in verse 40. There the preacher refers to God's provision of "something better with us in mind." The divine intention is that men and women of committed faith under the old covenant should not reach perfection "without us." The introduction of the plural pronouns in the first person, "with *us* in mind...without *us*," prepares for the transition to 12:1-3, where the pastor calls attention to the necessary endurance that must characterize the Christian community in its struggle with hostility and adversity.

In summary, 11:1-40 leads the audience into God's Hall of Fame. Here they listen to the roll-call of approved models of committed faithfulness who clarify for us the role of faith in the life of the man or woman of God. *They acted in their present in the light of the certainty of the promised future.* The promise extended to them could not be fulfilled apart from us. Although they experienced the fulfillment of specific promises in their lifetime, they did not attain the ultimate promise of the joy of final salvation. It is an expression of God's grace toward Christians that they should attain the promise only together with us. We are to be brought to the goal of faith together with them.

That encouragement provides the bridge from 11:1-40 to 12:1-3, where the preacher calls his friends to express the endurance which is the corollary of committed faith. The center of attention now shifts from the models of faithfulness in the distant and more recent past to a positive Christian response to the call for committed faith expressed through endurance.

The appeal is for the new people of God to demonstrate the same quality of committed faithfulness that is commended in the pages of Scripture and in the historical memory of Israel. The preacher uses the metaphor of the footrace to make his point:

Consequently, since we are surrounded by so great a multitude of witnesses, ridding ourselves of every burden, and the sin that is so prone to hamper us, let us run with endurance the race that lies before us (12:1).

The writer has in mind any encumbrance that would handicap a runner, and by analogy, anything that would hinder responsible commitment to Jesus Christ. In this way he sought to encourage his friends to free themselves from associations and engagements, however innocent in themselves, that would hamper their freedom for Christian action. The pastor was aware that in the footrace the competitors removed all of their clothing before running so that nothing could hinder them during the contest. In the same way, the Christian is to throw off everything which might stop him from serving God freely.

The further challenge to rid ourselves of *the sin* so prone to hamper shows that the pastor is thinking of *sin itself*, rather than of specific sins. Faith finds its essential character in commitment to God and to a life-style that reflects devotion to God.

Two encouragements are offered to those who listen to this sermon to press on in faith and obedience to the final goal.

(1) *The first encouragement is the certainty of being surrounded with a multitude of witnesses.* It is tempting to think of an amphitheater with its ascending rows of spectators who gather to watch the contest. But a witness is never merely a spectator. He is a participant who pledges his life to validate what he has seen and experienced. The emphasis in 12:1 thus falls on what Christians see in them, rather than on what they see in Christians. These witnesses are the men and women of Chapter 11 who have received acknowledgment from God because of their faith. They stand in Scripture as a witness to the character of committed faith and to the possibilities of faith for later generations. As such, they speak with a vibrant voice to believers in all ages.

(2) *The supreme encouragement springs from the contemplation of Jesus,* "the champion and perfecter of faith, who for the joy set before him endured the cross, thinking nothing of the shame" (12:2). The pastoral appeal is for a concentrated attention that looks away from the immediate surroundings, with eyes only for the person of Jesus. The use of the personal name "Jesus" shows that the focus should be upon his experiences as a man, and especially his endurance of pain, humiliation, and the shame of the cross. *Jesus is the ultimate witness to men and women of committed faith that God honors faithfulness.* His personal trust in God during the experience of his passion provides the supreme example of the life of committed faith.

The nature of Jesus' experience is sketched in verses 2-3. The way of the Son of God in the world is described as the way to the cross. Moreover, the death on the cross is understood from the viewpoint of humiliation, as the expression of shame and disgrace. *Christ was not free from the struggle that characterizes Christian life in a hostile society.* He experienced disgrace and violent opposition. Thus the contest in which Jesus engaged is compared with the contest in which the community of faith is engaged. *What the preacher emphasizes is Jesus' attitude in the experience of suffering, shame, and disgrace.*

Jesus' heavenly session at God's right hand is related to the race of faith which he has already finished, and which Christians must yet run. Those who keep their eyes fixed upon him will be prepared to model their conduct on the pattern of his earthly endurance. Whenever they begin to become weary with the demands of the contest, they are to reflect upon his enthronement at God's right hand, and the joy he obtained as a prize in the Father's presence. That joy is the reward of endurance. *Christ humiliated* is the "forerunner" (6:20) and example (12:2) for his people in the life of committed faith. *Christ enthroned* is the basis of assurance that his people will also be able to endure and to enter into the joy set before them.

The appeal expressed in 12:1-3 is to imitate Jesus' faith, trusting in him. In him we find the one in who faith was expressed heroically ("the champion") and in whom faith has reached its perfection ("the perfecter"). He goes ahead of all others in faith and enables them to emulate his example. *Jesus makes the life of committed faith possible.*

The preacher is a man with a pastor's heart. He knows that it is possible to be worn down by harsh circumstances. The contours and ridges of the life of faith can be eroded. That is why he brings this section of the sermon to a conclusion with one final appeal: "Consider the one who endured from sinners such antagonism against himself, so that you will not become weary and lose heart" (12:3). Jesus knows from his own experience that hostile opposition is a harsh reality in a fallen world. He endured jeers and taunts, flogging, and crucifixion by sinful men who despised him without cause. He is the supreme witness to the life of committed faith expressed through endurance and submission to the will of God. Christians must fix their eyes upon him and draw from his example the courage to display responsible Christian commitment in their situation.

In summary, in 11:1—12:3 faith is shown to be an orientation to the future. The forward-looking character of faith lends solidness to the realm of Christian hope. Faith celebrates now the reality of future blessings which are certain because they are grounded in the promise of God. For the Christian it is the future, not the past, that molds the present. The preacher confesses, and promotes, the intensity of faith as an effective force which directs Christian life to the future. For the person of committed faith, the future is no longer insecure.

The themes of pilgrimage, of sighting the goal but not attaining it, and of refusing to be satisfied with a worldly reward permit the writer to explore the relationship between faith and hope. He understands that a mind is capable of hoping because its consciousness can be shaped by an invisible, heavenly reality. This intuition is presupposed in the recital of actions regulated by an outlook upon the future which found its basis in a dynamic faith in God and in the reward he confers upon those who please him (11:6).

The reward is the portion of those who seek God himself. The firm expectation of the reward is a matter of unwavering hope in God who has disclosed the future through his word of promise. Committed faith holds on to the promise, even when the integrity of the promise is called into question by the evidence of harsh circumstances. Faith knows that the one who promised is himself faithful.

The most striking aspect of the exposition is the elaboration of the relationship between faith and suffering. It is an arresting fact that the individuals mentioned in this well-known digest of the history of Israel are those who exercised faith in the face of death. Almost without exception, the context links each of the examples in some way or another to the experience of death (11:4, 5, 7, 11-12, 13, 17-19, 20, 21, 22, 23, 25-26, 29, 30, 31, 33-34, 35-38; 12:2-3). Those for whom death is not specified in the context were exposed to severe trials or peril because they were faithful to God.

An ability to endure suffering and death presupposes a vital relationship to the unseen, heavenly world. This dimension of the recital of faith in action indicates that this sermon has been carefully composed to address a crisis of faith in the life of the Christian community. The men and women of the house-church had already experienced adversity, humiliation, loss of property, and imprisonment (10:32-34). The list of approved witnesses, composed of those who were their forebearers and of Jesus their Lord, was designed to strengthen them in their resolve to be faithful to God, even in the event of martyrdom.

XI

Committed Pilgrimage
(Hebrews 12:4—13:25)

In Hebrews it is plainly stated that Christians in this life have no enduring city; we are looking toward the City which is to come (13:14). The high degree of mobility which characterizes our contemporary society enables us to identify emotionally with this distinctive point of view. In our quest for the City of God we resemble the patriarchs, who were expecting and seeking a city, or a home (11:10, 14, 16). This quest, undertaken by God's people under both the old and the new covenants, cannot be in vain because God has prepared a city for them (11:16). That city is firmly established because God is its designer and builder (11:10). *The metaphor of the journey to the City of God characterizes men and women of committed faith as pilgrims, and the Christian life as commitment to pilgrimage.*

This theme is familiar to people in the English-speaking world through John Bunyan's classic allegory of the Christian life, *Pilgrim's Progress*, yet it is found in the New Testament only in Hebrews. Elsewhere Christians are described as aliens and strangers in the world (e.g., 1 Pet. 1:1; 2:11), but they are resident aliens dwelling for a time in a foreign land while they hold their citizenship elsewhere (cf. Phil. 3:20; James 1:1).

More than this is involved in Hebrews. Summarizing his appeal to the patriarchs as models of faith, the preacher comments:

All these persons...confessed that they were strangers and sojourners in the land. Now people who say such things show plainly that they are expecting intently a homeland of their own. If they had meant that country from which they had set out, they would have had opportunity to return. But as it is they were longing for a better homeland, in other words, a heavenly one (11:13-16).

In the same intense way that the patriarchs sought a homeland (11:14), Christians seek the City which is to come (13:14). *The people of God are called to be a pilgrim people.*

The theme of the Christian life as pilgrimage becomes important whenever we concern ourselves with the deeper spiritual life. The situation of the Church expresses the inherent tension between secularization and spiritual maturity. Secularization is accommodation to the world. It occurs whenever we become comfortable and complacent with our surroundings. We begin to lose a perspective on life as a stranger in Babylon. It is imperative for the man or woman of God to remember that Babylon is not holy and that Babylon is not home. We have here no enduring city. As pilgrims earnestly waiting for the disclosure of the City of God we spurn the city of man.

The formulation used by the preacher to express the pilgrim's disposition is descriptive of an active seeking: *"we seek after the city which is to come"* (13:14). Here is the litmus test of spirituality: are you actively looking forward to the appearance of the City of God? What do you care about profoundly? What do you think about when you are caught day-dreaming? Do you display a pilgrim's disposition, actively seeking the City of God?

This perspective implies that for now home is wherever God would have us to be, but ultimately home is the unmediated presence of God himself. Materialism is the basic desire to accumulate material possessions and wealth. In a culture committed to materialism pilgrims are identified by their readiness to travel lightly. A pilgrim is necessarily lean and tough in spirit. His life is characterized by mobility; he is on the move. He remembers that the goal of pilgrimage is the City of God. The assurance of Hebrews is that we have a City (11:16). The future is certain. That perspective calls for an understanding of Christian life as commitment to pilgrimage.

This perspective sheds light on the concluding division of the sermon, 12:4—13:21. The structure of the development can be outlined.

A	Disciplinary sufferings and pilgrimage	(12:4-13)
B	Pilgrimage to the City of God	(12:14-29)
C	Mandates for pilgrims	(13:1-19)
D	Concluding benediction upon the pilgrim people	(13:20-21)
	Postscript	(13:22-25)

The factor that unites the several sections of 12:4—13:21 is the theme of committed pilgrimage.

Pilgrimage calls for a disciplined life. Simply defined, discipline is training. The Greek term for discipline, *paideia*, can have reference to training through education or training through chastening. Discipline is education by correction. It is always a reflection of one's education, initially in the home, and then subsequently in school, as diligence is encouraged and rewarded, and irresponsibility is exposed and punished. It is natural to refer to family relationships when speaking about discipline, for our experience of parental discipline is intended to prepare us to recognize the crucial factor of divine discipline. We discover that relationships within a family can help us to understand and appreciate God's relationship to us.

In Hebrews 12:4-13 the preacher refers to *disciplinary sufferings* and relates them to the theme of pilgrimage. The expression "disciplinary sufferings" has reference to actual sufferings, which may be inflicted by those who are hostile toward God and who find in the people of God a target for their hostility. These sufferings become "disciplinary" when God makes them a means for leading his people to spiritual maturity. It is God's ability to transform an expression of hostility into a measure for spiritual nurture that is emphasized by the writer.

The pastor appreciates that Christians, at least to some extent, are involved in the same struggle in which Jesus engaged. His endurance of unjustified antagonism and his voluntary submission to humiliation and shame offers a model for Christians whenever they are tempted to become weary or disheartened with the opposition they encounter in a hostile society (12:3). There was, of course, both a qualitative and quantitative difference between the sufferings endured by Jesus, and those experienced by the Christians addressed in this sermon. The preacher candidly reminds his friends that they had "not yet resisted to the point of bloodshed struggling against sin" (12:4). Jesus had endured the excruciating pain and the shame of the Cross; they had not yet been subjected to such humiliation. But the difference was one of degree. They had experienced hostility, abuse, and suffering because they had openly identified themselves with Christ (10:32-34).

The deeper problem was that the members of the house-church had forgotten completely the biblical concept of disciplinary sufferings. The pastor urges his friends to regard their experience of suffering and deprivation as evidence that God recognized them as true sons and daughters. The sufferings they were enduring were actually disciplinary in character; they were a means of training them for a life of godliness appropriate to members of God's family. *In fact, their sufferings were an indispensable element in preparing them for a life of committed pilgrimage.*

The link between 12:1-3, where the preacher focuses upon Jesus' endurance of redemptive sufferings, and 12:4-13, where Christians are called to endure disciplinary sufferings, is the call not to lose heart.

Consider [Jesus] who endured from sinners such antagonism against himself, so that you may not become weary *and lose heart (12:3).*

And you have forgotten completely the exhortation which addresses you as sons, "My son, do not disregard the discipline of the Lord, and *do not lose heart* from his reprimand" (12:5).

The same thought is expressed metaphorically in the admonition in 12:12: "Therefore, brace up your listless arms and weak knees." The descriptive phrases, "listless arms" and "weak knees," evoke the picture of a person who is thoroughly discouraged. The phrases describe those who have lost heart. Pilgrimage demands heart. The preacher recognizes this fact in the repeated appeal not to lose heart.

In this initial section (12:4-13) the pastor emphasizes the importance of divine discipline, the purpose of divine discipline, and the proper response to divine discipline. He describes the teaching of Scripture concerning divine discipline as a "word of exhortation" or a "word of encouragement" (v. 5). The note of encouragement is found in the fact that God acknowledges us as *his children*. We are addressed as sons and daughters in the authoritative word cited from Proverbs 3:11-12:

My child, do not disregard the discipline of the Lord, and do not lost heart from his reprimand; for the Lord disciplines the one whom he loves, and scourges every child whom he accepts (vv. 5-6).

That instruction was easily forgotten in the experience of suffering. It is, nevertheless, a word of encouragement because we are addressed as members of God's family. The experience of disciplinary sufferings affirms that we have been accepted as sons and daughters of God.

In this unit, then, the preacher called his friends to endure hardship as family discipline (v. 7). Lack of discipline in a family would actually be an indication of abandonment by a father (v. 8). The pastor appeals to the common experience that children are disciplined by their parents, and observes, We respected them for this. But divine discipline is more necessary than ordinary parental discipline because God is training us for life with himself and with each other. The preacher writes: "Then again, we have had human fathers who disciplined us, and we have respected them. Should we not much more submit ourselves to the Father of spirits so that we shall live?" (v. 9). *The appeal to our experience in the home underscores the importance of divine discipline.*

The purpose of divine discipline is elaborated in the distinction drawn between parental discipline and divine discipline: "For Our fathers disciplined us for a short time as seemed good to them, but God [disciplines us] for our benefit in order that we might share in his holiness" (v. 10). Our parent's discipline was imperfect. It originated often in anger. At times it was unjust. But God's discipline is perfect for its goal is to bring us to spiritual maturity and to prepare us to share in his holiness! The clear implication of verse 10 is that it is impossible to share in God's holiness apart from the correction administered through disciplinary sufferings, which have the effect of maturing us as men and women of God.

The preacher frankly acknowledges that disciplinary suffering is unpleasant, but its intention is a harvest of righteousness and peace for those who have been trained by this form of correction (v. 11). The prospect of "a peaceful harvest of righteousness" is an occasion for joy. The preacher asserts that joy is the prospect of Christians after painful discipline, just as joy was the prospect placed before Christ after he had endured the painful opposition of sinful men (12:2-3).

The appropriate response to divine discipline is renewed resolve to prepare to engage in a demanding contest: "Therefore, brace up your listless arms and weak knees, and make straight paths for your feet, so that the lame limb not be put out of joint but rather healed" (vv. 12-13). The thought of training through disciplinary sufferings in verse 11 suggests the metaphor of an athletic contest requiring flexed arms and strong knees. We are to ready ourselves for the contest (cf. 12:1), bracing our listless arms and weak knees. We are to clear out the clutter from our lives, making a level path for our feet, so that we will incur no injury. The imagery is enriched from another passage in Proverbs which the writer evidently recalled:

> My child...let your eyes look straight ahead,
> fix your gaze directly before you.
> Make level paths for your feet
> and take only ways that are firm.
> Do not swerve to the right or to the left;
> keep your feet from evil
> (Prov. 4:25-27).

The instruction is appropriate for a person who is about to enter a race or to undertake a journey to a fixed destination.

It is the thought of the journey that indicates how the matter of disciplinary sufferings is related to the theme of pilgrimage. The pilgrim must brace up listless arms and weak knees because the pilgrimage may be long and the journey arduous. It is the pilgrim who must make level paths for his feet, not swerving from the road that will lead him to his determined destination. Those whose limbs are lame cannot engage in pilgrimage. Men and women who are prepared to heed the pastor's instruction, however, have the prospect that even the lame will not be disabled but will experience the healing that God gives to those who fix their eyes upon the goal of the City of God.

According to Hebrews 12:4-13, then, the goal of discipline is Christian maturity and, ultimately, participation in the holiness of God. Those who willingly submit to disciplinary sufferings participate in the triumph of the cross of Christ. The implication that the preacher wanted his friends to draw from these facts is clear: *those who attempt to humliate the people of God by the infliction of painful sufferings cannot frustrate the divine purpose which is motivated by the Father's love for his children.* Whenever we experience unpleasantness, pain, and hardship because we are Christians, we can recognize tokens of the Father's love. We can also recognize a call to strengthen our resolve to engage in pilgrimage to the heavenly City of God.

The theme of pilgrimage to the City of God is more sharply expressed in the following section, 12:14-29. Here the preacher compares the experience of Israel, on pilgrimage to Mount Sinai, with the experience of the Church on pilgrimage to the City of God. Prior to elaborating upon details which illumine the goal of pilgrimage, however, he addresses the issue of priorities for pilgrims in verses 14-17. A priority is a primary concern in the life of a believer.

The issue of establishing priorities is always troublesome. Charles Hummel comments upon this fact in a significant pamphlet entitled, *The Tyranny of the Urgent*. He observed that matters of crucial importance can be pushed aside simply because urgent concerns demand our attention. *Priorities are always a matter of commitment, and a measure of maturity.*

Committed pilgrimage necessarily entails a concern with priorities. The pastor knows from experience that spiritual maturity does not evolve by itself. It is cultivated in response to the establishing of certain primary concerns. It is developed because a Christian has made the attainment of spiritual maturity a priority in his or her life.

The pastor brings before his friends a series of seemingly simple instructions in verses 14-17. For example, "Pursue peace with everyone, and the holiness without which no one will see the Lord" (v. 14). The formulation appears to be so general in character that it is easily relegated to the realm of the forgotten. The set of instructions in verses 14-17 is seldom made the subject for deep reflection or for teaching in the Church. That may be one reason why there is so little evidence of spiritual maturity in the Church. As a unit, verses 14-17 are followed immediately by verses 18-24, which define the goal of pilgrimage in explicit terms. It is clear, therefore, that the instructions set forth in verses 14-17 have been framed with commitment to pilgrimage in mind.

The instruction consists of two positive commands and two negative commands. It will be easier to grasp what the preacher said to his friends by reducing all four commands to a positive formulation. *These verses address matters important to those who are committed to pilgrimage.*

(1) *Make every effort to live in peace with all persons* (v. 14a). This advice follows upon a section in which the pastor spoke of enduring antagonism from sinful men (12:3) and of resisting opposition to the extent of martyrdom (12:4). A vital Christian presence can provoke conflict within a pagan society, because Christians call into question the values of a pagan society. Nevertheless, the Christian pilgrim is to seek to cultivate a peaceful relationship with all persons. This is a matter of commending the gospel to our neighbors by a disposition of openness to other persons.

(2) *Make every effort to be holy* (v. 14b). It is clear that this admonition imposes a limitation upon the instruction to cultivate a peaceful relationship with everyone (v. 14a). There can be no compromise with Christian principles in seeking to cultivate a

pagan society for the gospel of Christ. This instruction provides a sober reminder that Christians serve a holy God, who is creating for himself a holy people. His intention is that we shall share in his holiness (12:10). The final goal of pilgrimage is the vision of God, and this vision is the privilege solely of those whose lives assume the character trait of holiness (12:14).

This admonition elaborates the emphasis the preacher had developed in the central core of the sermon.

We have been made holy through the sacrifice of the body of Jesus Christ once for all (10:10).
By one sacrifice he has made perfect forever *those who are being made holy* (10:14).

Christians are made holy and are consecrated to the service of God through the effective power of Christ's death on the Cross. They are to participate in the process of being made holy by cultivating a life-style that is pleasing to God. When the preacher instructs his friends to "pursue the holiness without which no one will see the Lord" he is urging them to reflect the essential quality of the Father so that a pagan society will recognize in them the family likeness!

(3) *Make every effort to cultivate the grace of God* (v. 15). Here a positive reformulation brings out the intention of the text: "Watch that no one misses the grace of God and that no root of bitterness spring up to cause trouble and many be defiled through it" (v. 15). The implication of the preacher's instruction is that unless Christians are actively seeking to be sensitive to the grace of God, the tokens of his gracious disposition toward his children will not be recognized. This admonition calls for an alertness that God's gifts are frequently experienced in the form of an unanticipated surprise. The sheer delight they bring can provide us with an occasion for spontaneous praise. There will be no place for bitterness when a Christian pilgrim discovers that he is sustained by the pervasive presence of the grace of God.

A spirit of bitterness breeds bitterness and trouble; it possesses the ability to contaminate many persons. Bitterness spoils relationships. It defiles the human spirit. God's response to an embittered spirit is the outpouring of grace. Those committed to pilgrimage must make a priority of cultivating the grace of God.

(4) *Make every effort to be sexually responsible* (vv. 16-17). In this instance, too, it is helpful to invert a prohibition and reformulate it as a positive command:

Watch that no one becomes sexually immoral or godless like Esau, who in exchange for one dish of food sold his birthrights as the eldest son. For you know that later on when he wished to inherit the blessing he was rejected, for he could bring about no change of mind [on the part of Isaac], although he pleaded for the blessing with tears (vv. 16-17).

Sexual immorality is actually a rejection of the presence and goodness of God who created us in our maleness and femaleness. It is an expression of a selfishness that is blind to the emotional fragileness that characterizes each one of us.

Sexual responsibility is an awareness that our human sexuality is the gift of God. It is to be respected as an expression of our distinctiveness as persons. Sexual responsibility is an opportunity to affirm the lordship of God the Creator in the pilgrim's life. That is why the pastor counsels the men and women of the house-church, "Watch that no one become sexually immoral" (v. 16*a*; cf. 13:4).

The related command is to watch that no one become "godless like Esau" (v. 16*b*). A godless person is one who allows his appetities to dictate his desires and his behavior. He is godless because he enthrones his appetites as god! Such a person was Esau, whose decision to exchange his inheritance rights as the eldest son for a full stomach (Gen. 25:29-34) illustrates the folly of decisions of the moment.

These *four instructions* define priorities for all who make a commitment to pilgrimage: *a peaceful disposition, holiness of life, an active sense of the grace of God, and moral responsibility.* That these are matters of concern related to pilgrimage becomes evident in verses 18-24, when the goal of completed pilgrimage is described.

The pastor addresses the goal of pilgrimage first negatively, by contrasting the experience of the Church with that of Israel after the exodus from Egypt:

For you have not come to a mountain that is material and burning with fire, and to darkness and gloom and whirlwind; and to a trumpet blast and a voice speaking words, that those who heard it begged not to add another word to them.... The spectacle was so awesome that Moses said, "I am terrified and trembling" (vv. 18-21).

The description refers to Mount Sinai, the goal of Israel's pilgrimage into the wilderness, where God entered into solemn covenant with them. There Israel discovered the awesomeness and the terrifying reality of relationship with a transcendent, holy God.

The goal of Christian pilgrimage is described in very different terms:

> But you have come to Mount Zion and to the City of the living God, to heavenly Jerusalem, and to myriads of angels, to a festal gathering, and to the assembly of the firstborn whose names are recorded in heaven, and to God, the judge of all men, and to the spirits of righteous men made perfect, and to Jesus, the mediator of a new covenant, and to the sprinkled blood that speaks to more purpose than the blood of Abel (vv. 22-24).

Here the preacher describes the final goal of committed pilgrimage, arrival at the City of God, where angels gather in festal assembly with the redeemed of all ages because pilgrimage has been completed. These verses reflect a vision of what it will mean for all of God's people to be gathered together in the presence of God, when we shall see Jesus, the mediator of the new covenant, and will experience the inexpressible reality of the death of Christ which cries for redemption rather than vengeance.

The vision of arrival at the City of God poses for Christians a crucial issue: What is real? What is real to you? So long as Christians live as if the real is what can be touched, tasted, and grasped with the senses, as opposed to the realm of the spiritual which must be grasped by faith, they will not mature. *Our attitude toward reality tends to reflect another aspect of the materialism which effects us so profoundly.* If something lacks materiality, so that it cannot be grasped in a tangible way, we tend to dismiss its reality. That is why the preacher deliberately contrasts Mount Sinai, a mountain that is material, with Mount Zion, the City of God and heavenly Jerusalem. *Hebrews affirms that the greatest expression of reality is God and the assembly of those who gather in his presence.* When we come to the City of God we come to Jesus Christ, the mediator of the new covenant. That helps us to resolve the issue of what is real: *we come to him who is real!*

The preacher wanted his friends to cultivate a sense of their participation in reality already at that point in their experience. He writes, *"You have come* to Mount Zion and to the City of the living God!"* (v. 22). *We have come* to the great future assembly! For Christians the formulation poses a series of urgent questions: are you aware of your participation in the total assembly of God's people, in the gathering of all of the men and women of faith who have preceded you? Do you know that you are the heir to their prayers, their labors, their sufferings, and their dreams? Growth in spirituality depends upon corporate growth with all the people of God. We grow together as we move out in committed pilgrimage together, anticipating the excitement and fulfillment of the arrival at the City of God and the completion of pilgrimage.

The vitality of the vision of completed pilgrimage clarifies the urgency of the climactic admonition in this section: "See that you do not disregard the one who is speaking. For if [Israel] did not escape when they disregarded the one who warned them on earth, how much less will we, if we turn away from the one who warns us from heaven?" (v. 25). This warning is uttered in the light of God's promise to shake all of creation at the end of the age (v. 26). When Israel gathered at the base of Mount Sinai, the earth shook at the voice of the Lord. But at the consummation of history the heavens will be shaken as well. *A commitment to pilgrimage is the only hope of enduring the time of shaking,* for the purpose of pilgrimage is arrival at the City that possesses foundations which cannot be shaken (12:28; 13:14). Then the hardships of pilgrimage will be past. Faith, the present grasp of invisible truth, will be exchanged for sight, and Christians will discover that God delights himself in his pilgrim people. That is the vision held out to the new people of God by the pastor.

The section is brought to a conclusion on a strong note of encouragement: "Therefore, since we are receiving a kingdom which cannot be shaken, let us be grateful, and through gratitude let us worship God acceptably with reverence and awe; for our God is a consuming fire" (vv. 28-29). The cultivation of a sense of gratitude and of sustained worship are expressions of a commitment to the pilgrim's disposition in a world that is insensitive to the reality and awesome holiness of God.

Pilgrimage thus proves to be an expressive metaphor for a lifestyle molded by the vision of the City of God. It implies that the tensions now existing between promise and fulfillment will be resolved in the presence of God and the festal assembly of angels together with the company of the redeemed. It calls the men and women of the house-church to look beyond the experience of suffering in the world to the heavenly Jerusalem in anticipation of their vindication as the children of God and heirs to an inexpressible salvation. It invites them to act on the realization that even now they share by faith in the awesome reality which can only be suggested by the vision of completed pilgrimage in the presence of the God who is real.

In the concluding portion of the sermon (13:1-21) the preacher brings together *a collection of mandates for pilgrims.* He recognizes a need to remind his friends in the house-church of certain elementary Christian virtues. These must not be neglected in their concentration upon the demands imposed by pilgrimage. The series of mandates expose specific commitments which are appropriate to a pilgrim people of God.

The mandates are introduced with the admonition, "Let brotherly love continue" (13:1). The instructions which follow in Chapter 13 clarify related aspects of this fundamental mandate.

(1) *Practice hospitality as an expression of brotherly love* ("Do not neglect hospitality," v. 2). A commitment to hospitality was of crucial importance to the success of the early Christian mission. Christian preachers and teachers who travelled from one center to the next depended upon the openness of Christian homes for shelter during the night and the provision of food for the next day's labor (cf. 3 John 3-8). An expression of hospitality was often the meal, as an occasion for refreshment and the sharing of Christian love with those who were not in a position to reciprocate the kindness in any direct way. The preacher was convinced that Christians neglect hospitality at the cost of a blessing.

He may well have known the tradition of Jesus' words, as recorded in the Parable of the Sheep and the Goats (Matt. 25:31-46):

> I was hungry, and you gave me food,
> I was thirsty, and you gave me drink,
> I was a stranger, and you welcomed me
> (Matt. 25:35).

And when the surprised people ask, "Lord, when did we see you hungry and feed you or thirsty and give you something to drink?" he will reply, "Whatever you did for these brothers and sisters of mine, you did for me" (Matt. 25:37, 40). But there will be another group of persons gathered before the King, to whom he will say:

> I was hungry, and you gave me nothing to eat,
> I was thirsty, and you gave me nothing to drink,
> I was a stranger, and you did not invite me in
> (Matt. 25:42).

When those shocked Christians protest, "When did we see you hungry or thirsty or a stranger?" he will reply, "Whatever you did not do for one of the least of these others, you did not do for me" (Matt. 25:42, 45). Hospitality is an expression of love for Jesus which meets the needs of his brothers and sisters.

The mandate not to neglect hospitality is a plea for unselfishness. In Hebrews it is supported by an appeal to the hospitable disposition of Abraham, who entertained angels without being aware of the fact (cf. Gen. 18:1-8). The allusion to Abraham is significant because *he was himself a man on pilgrimage to the City of God! Hospitality is a pilgrim virtue.*

(2) *Demonstrate a practical concern for others as an expression of brotherly love* ("Remember the prisoners as if you were their fellow prisoners, and those who are mistreated as being also yourselves in the body [and so liable to the same treatment]," v. 3). The preacher calls upon his friends to demonstrate a genuine empathy for those who were imprisoned; they are to remember the prisoners as if they were in prison themselves! This had been a hallmark of the love they had demonstrated in the early days of their experience as Christians, when they "had compassion on the prisoners" (10:34). In the ancient world prisoners had to depend upon family and friends for their meals and for any measures of emotional support to help them endure the unsavory conditions of imprisonment. Christians were distinguished for the quality of the concern they manifested for brothers and sisters who had been imprisoned. That concern was authorized by Jesus' words, "I was in prison, and you visited me" (Matt. 25:36), but it was also an expression of love for one another. The writer's own commitment to this mandate finds expression at the conclusion of Hebrews, when he shares with his friends the good news "that our brother Timothy has been set free [from prison], in whose company, if he comes soon, I will see you" (13:23).

Empathy must also be extended to the mistreated—the abused, the deprived, those who have experienced little or no kindness in their lives. This mandate corresponds to Jesus' words, "I was naked, and you clothed me, I was sick, and you visited me" (Matt. 25:36). The naked were the mistreated; the sick were too often those who were neglected and shunned. In reference to an earlier experience of hostile treatment from their society the pastor recalled that these men and women "were sometimes exposed to abuse and affliction, and sometimes were partners with those who were mistreated in this way" (10:32). The striking fact is that this instance of Christian empathy was the response to those who experienced pilgrimage in the form of banishment from Rome under an imperial edict (cf. Acts 18:1-2).

(3) *Cultivate fidelity in marriage as an expression of brotherly love* ("Marriage should be respected by everyone, and the marriage-bed undefiled, for God will judge those who are sexually immoral and adulterers" v. 4.) This mandate addresses both the married and those who are unmarried: let marriage be highly esteemed; let the marriage-bed be respected by all persons. The pastor appreciated the fact that attitudes formed and expressed prior to marriage will inevitable affect attitudes and dispositions displayed in the course of marriage. Christians found in marriage an opportunity to experience the full maturing of affection and the mutual support that God intended for his children. It is also an expression of brotherly love, for Christian marriage will display how profoundly we love our closest brother or sister in the Lord!

The warning that God will judge the sexually immoral person and the adulterer is also a word to the married and the unmarried. Its ground is the biblical conception that marriage is a creation ordinance of God; it has been the gift of God to the human family from the time of the creation of human life. Marriage thus becomes the sphere in which Christians will invariably display the degree of seriousness with which they regard God as Creator and his mandates concerning marriage. A cultivation of fidelity in marriage will release married couples and single persons alike to pursue pilgrimage in an atmosphere of mutual support and delight.

(4) *Preserve a freedom from greed as an expression of brotherly love* ("Keep your manner of life free from the love of money; be content with what you have, because God himself has said, 'I will never fail you; I will never forsake you,'" v. 5). The preacher called his friends to experience the freedom of a life unhampered by the love of money. He recognized that the concern for profit which motivated all business enterprise in the ancient world represented a subtle conformity to the world. It encouraged a grasping disposition and a self-centeredness which was a denial of the experience of brotherly love. This remains true of our own society as well. A pilgrim, by definition, is one who is committed to travelling with few possessions. His commitment to a life of simplicity is the source of deep contentment with what he has. He is motivated not by a desire to accumulate material goods and tokens of status but by the vision of arrival at the City of God. This vision calls him to pilgrimage as a life-style.

Deep contentment is simply quietness in your situation. Its

condition is reliance upon God who has promised his presence with us. The preacher recalls for his friends the assurance that God gave to his pilgrim people under Moses, "I will never fail you, I will never forsake you" (Deut. 31:6). The promise of God's unfailing presence implies that he engages in pilgrimage with his pilgrim people! That recognition encourages Christians to risk the rigors of pilgrimage without fear: "So undaunted we say, 'The Lord is my helper: I will not be afraid. What can man do to me?' " (v. 6). The pilgrim people find themselves sustained by the presence of their God who shares a commitment to pilgrimage.

(5) *Respect those in authority as an expression of brotherly love* ("Remember your leaders, as those who spoke the word of God to you. Consider the outcome of their way of life and imitate their faith....Obey your leaders, and submit to their authority, for they keep watch over you as those who must render an account. Obey them so that they may do this with joy...Pray for us," vv. 7, 17-19). The responsibility of a pilgrim people is respect for those who have been appointed to leadership in the Church, imitation of their godly lives, support of their various ministries, and earnest prayer for their integrity. The responsibility of the leaders is the sharing of the word of God, deep faith, diligence in the fulfillment of their ministries, a clear conscience, and responsible behavior. Neither the pilgrim people nor their leaders may relax their vigilance for a moment, for together they will display to their world the character of Christian commitment and the quality of brotherly love.

(6) *Celebrate the praise of God as an expression of brotherly love* ("Therefore, let us through [Jesus] continually offer a sacrifice consisting in praise....Do not neglect acts of kindness and sharing with others, for God is pleased with such sacrifices," vv. 15-16). The praise of God, defined as "the fruit of lips that confess his name" (v. 15*b*), must be complemented by a life-style characterized by generosity and brotherly love. These related aspects of the pilgrim disposition are linked together by the category of sacrifice. Through Jesus, the sufficient sacrifice for sin (13:11-13), Christians offer to God the sacrifice of praise and the well-pleasing sacrifices of love and the nurture of others. Without the praise of God, acts of kindness and of sharing would be little more than joyless humanitarianism. Without acts of kindness

and of sharing, the praise of God would be empty formalism. Both praise and love are indispensable to the life of Christian pilgrimage.

These mandates are undergirded by two powerful supports provided to the pilgrim people of God. In the course of pilgrimage they will be supported by the unconditional character of the divine promises and by the unchanging character of Jesus Christ.

(1) *The unconditional promise of God is the solemn pledge of his presence*: "I will never fail you; I will never forsake you" (v. 5). God identifies himself with his people and will never abandon them to their own limited resources. The emotions of fear, panic, discouragement, and despair would be appropriate if Christians were called to pilgrimage in the absence of God. The experience of his promised presence, however, justifies the confident affirmation, "The Lord is my helper; I will not be afraid! What can man do to me?" (v. 6).

(2) *The unchanging character of Jesus Christ is the solemn pledge of his firm commitment to his people*. In the course of enumerating the mandates for pilgrims the preacher utters a shout of celebration, "Jesus Christ is the same yesterday, and today, and forever" (v. 8). This is the presupposition for commitment to pilgrimage. The conditions of pilgrimage may change, but he abides constant. Wherever the pilgrim people may go, they may be confident that they are in the presence of the one who remains consistently the same. Their circumstances may be altered; he does not change. In a society characterized by instability, he remains the source of firm stability. He identified himself with his brothers and sisters "yesterday" most profoundly in his death upon the cross. He continued to identify himself with them "today" in the crisis of renewed hostility and persecution. He will be with the pilgrim people of God "forever," as the expression of an undeviating concern for their welfare.

The sermon is brought to a conclusion formally with a benediction which evokes the thought of pilgrimage in a striking way:

May the God of peace, who through the blood of the eternal covenant brought up from the dead our Lord Jesus, that great Shepherd of the sheep, equip you with everything good for doing his will, and may he accomplish in us what is pleasing in his sight through Jesus Christ, to whom be glory forever and ever. Amen (vv. 20-21).

The references to "the blood of the eternal covenant" and to the "doing" of God's will effectively summarize the heart of the preacher's message to his friends. But they are left finally, with the representation of Jesus as "the great shepherd of the sheep." The image is thoroughly satisfying. It recalls the pilgrim experience of Israel during the period of the exodus from Egypt and the crossing of the sea:

> Then his people recalled the days of old,
>   the days of Moses and his people—
> where he is who brought them through the sea,
>   with the shepherd of his flock? (Isa. 63:11)

The image of the shepherd leading the flock that follows him wherever he goes is appropriate to the theme of commitment to pilgrimage. Under the old covenant, the pilgrim people of God were to find in Moses "the shepherd of the flock." But under the new covenant, inaugurated through "the blood of the eternal covenant," the new pilgrim people are led by the great shepherd, the Lord Jesus, whom God brought up from the dead. The prayer for the accomplishment of what is pleasing in God's sight through Jesus Christ finds an appropriate response in the commitment of the Church to pilgrimage.

Afterword

The preacher responsible for Hebrews was eager to support his friends not simply with the sermon he prepared but with his presence as well. In a brief personal remark appended to the sermon he informed them that he was planning to visit them soon (13:23). He urged them to pray specifically that he might be restored to them shortly (13:19). He was convinced that his personal presence would do much to strengthen the resolve of the house-church to remain loyal to Christ, even if the price of fidelity was martyrdom. He undoubtedly hoped that his arrival would stem the tide of defections which had disrupted the assembly.

We do not know whether the pastor ever arrived in Rome and was able to minister to his friends as he desired. It is also impossible to know the extent to which the house-church was directly affected by the measures taken by Nero against Christians in the imperial capital. We do know that the suffering Church in Rome survived Nero's persecution, and experienced growth in numbers, influence, and spiritual maturity. *It is certain that the sermon prepared by the pastor was a significant factor in the survival of the church in Rome.*

Evidence of the impact of Hebrews upon the life of the larger church in Rome is provided by an early Christian document known as *1 Clement*. This is a pastoral letter sent by the church in Rome to the sister church of Corinth which was experiencing disruption during the final decade of the first Christian century. It is usually dated AD 95, some thirty years after the composition of Hebrews. Although the actual name of the writer is not mentioned in the letter itself, an unbroken tradition ascribes it to Clement, a senior pastor of the church in Rome during the last decades of the first century.

177

Clement provides indisputable evidence that Hebrews was known and treasured in the churches of Rome during this period. Not only are there striking parallels to the form and statement of Hebrews throughout the letter, but Clement actually quotes Hebrews in the context of the distinctive teaching that Jesus is our high priest.

One example will be sufficient to suggest the extent of the knowledge of Hebrews reflected in *1 Clement*:

This is the way, beloved, in which we found our salvation, Jesus Christ, the high priest of our offerings, the defender and helper of our weaknesses... "who being the radiance of his Majesty is so much greater than the angels as he has inherited a more excellent name." For it is written, "who makes his angels spirits, and his ministers a flame of fire." But of the Son the Master said, "You are my son. Today I have become your father. Ask me, and I will give you the nations for your inheritance, and the ends of the earth for your possession." And again he says to him, "Sit at my right hand until I make your enemies a stool for your feet" (*1 Clement* 36:1-6).

The designation of Jesus as "high priest" and as "defender and helper of our weaknesses" (cf. Heb. 2:17-18; 4:15-16) occurs in a paragraph that looks like a patchwork of phrases culled from Hebrews 1:3-13. In fact, the descriptive clause, "who being the radiance of his Majesty is so much greater than the angels as he has inherited a more excellent name," is clearly a quotation summarizing Hebrews 1:3-4.

Moreover, when Clement quotes Psalm 110:1 as a direct word of address by God to the Son, as in Hebrews 1:13, he shows his dependence upon Hebrews' formula of introduction. This manner of introducing Old Testament quotations is typical of Hebrews (1:5-13; 5:5-16; 7:17, 21) but occurs only here in *1 Clement*.

A final consideration is relevant. The chain of Old Testament citations brought together by Clement would encourage a writer to designate Jesus as the Son, not "high priest." It is the presentation of God's Son as high priest in Hebrews which encouraged Clement to link his paraphrase of Hebrews 1 with Jesus' high priestly ministry and to further qualify him as "the defender and helper of our weaknesses."

Clement clearly knew the detail of Hebrews and drew upon its distinctive presentation of Jesus as God's Son and high priest. The manner in which he used Hebrew shows that he fully recognized the authority of Hebrews. There can be no doubt that the sermon had a wholesome impact upon the theology of the Church in Rome and that it fulfilled an important pastoral role by sustaining the Church through the periods of persecution and consolidation which followed.

Then for some unexplained reason Hebrews experienced an extended period of neglect. It was seldom cited in the second and third century, as the Church contented itself with other documents of the New Testament. Infrequent references to Hebrews show that some church leaders questioned its authority. Apparently, divergent points of view over the authorship of Hebrews kept the Church from listening to the content of the sermon. For all intents and purposes, Hebrews was lost to the Church. When it was rediscovered and its authority was recognized once again in the fourth century it was acknowledged to belong to the canon of Scripture, but there is little evidence that it exercised any considerable influence upon the thought and life of the Church.

Vital impact followed by an extended period of neglect appears to have been characteristic of Hebrews. The pattern emerging from the early Church brings us full circle to the contemporary neglect of this significant presentation of Christ as champion and priest, and of the Christian life as the celebration of worship or as pilgrimage to the City of God. The neglect of Hebrews exposes the Church to many of the perils about which the pastor was concerned to warn his friends, and it suppresses the promises with which he sought to support them in their own commitment to responsible discipleship. A rediscovery of Hebrews by the contemporary Church will be the source of fresh perspectives from which to approach obedience and mission in a materialistic and indifferent society. The call to commitment that is issued by this sermon for the Christian pilgrim must be proclaimed with renewed intensity.

Index